Body Image Breakthrough

"Women are constantly at war with themselves and the image they see in the mirror. This book offers down-to-earth insights and heavenly tools for LDS women to gain ground in their battle against negative body image."

—Betsy Schow, TODAY Show featured author of *Finished Being Fat: An Accidental Adventure in Losing Weight and Learning to Finish*

"*Body Image Breakthrough* gives wonderful insight into a topic we can all relate to. With humor and plain speaking, Jaci Wightman tackles this subject in a way that will benefit all readers. I thoroughly enjoyed reading this addition to the subject of body image."

—LeAnne W. Tolley, ERYT, CHES, author of *JUST LET GO!*

"*Body Image Breakthrough* is truly that, a breakthrough beyond the cliche 'just love your body.' Jaci magically opens up a whole new understanding of the issues with body worship not only in today's society, but also digs into its roots in ancient times. Jaci's depth of scriptural explanation and insights into the crazy and warped way in which we worship the ideal body image is unparalleled in this realm. She truly will help you see yourself in a whole new light and help open your eyes to the wonderful creation that you are. This book is a must-read to anyone who has a body!"

—Jen Brewer, RD, author of *Be the Chocolate Chip, Stop Dieting and Start Losing Weight*, and *We Are Daughters*

JACI WIGHTMAN

CFI
An imprint of Cedar Fort, Inc.
Springville, Utah

ISBN 13: 978-1-4621-1438-2

Published by CFI, an imprint of Cedar Fort, Inc.
2373 W. 700 S., Springville, UT, 84663
Distributed by Cedar Fort, Inc., www.cedarfort.com

LIBRARY OF CONGRESS CATALOGING-IN-PUBLICATION DATA

Wightman, Jaci, 1971- author.
Body image breakthrough / Jaci Wightman.
    pages cm
Includes bibliographical references and index.
ISBN 978-1-4621-1438-2 (alk. paper)
1. Body image in women--Religious aspects--Church of Jesus Christ of Latter-day Saints. 2. Mormon women--Conduct of life. I. Title.

BF697.5.B63W536 2014
306.4'613--dc23

                              2014004560

Cover design by Shawnda T. Craig
Cover design © 2014 Lyle Mortimer
Edited and typeset by Jessica B. Ellingson

Printed in the United States of America

10   9   8   7   6   5   4   3   2   1

Printed on acid-free paper

For my girls, Shay, Kalli, and Lexi,
who radiate the beauty of the Lord
both inside and out

Contents

Acknowledgments

To the entire crew at Cedar Fort—Catherine, Emily, Jessica, Kelly, Rebecca, Shawnda, and any others who helped make this book a reality: Thank you for being so wonderful. You've truly been a joy to work with from start to finish.

To my sister-in-law, Desi Wightman: Only you and I know the countless hours you've spent teaching me how to write. I never, ever could have done it without you. A profound thank-you from the very bottom of my heart.

To Breck and Katelyn, Kyler, Chase, Shay, Kimball, Kalli, and Lexi: Your support and encouragement have meant the world to me. Being your mom has been the greatest adventure ever. I love you all so much.

To my husband, Greg: Your influence has changed my life in a thousand ways. Thank you for your patience with me. Not only have you captured my heart, but even better, after twenty-four years, you can still make me laugh.

And finally, to my precious Savior, I echo the words of Nephi: "The Lord Jehovah is my strength and my song; he has also become my salvation." With my whole soul, I long to "cry out and shout," and to "praise the Lord" and "declare his doings among the people" (2 Nephi 22:2–6). I hope this book does exactly that.

The Ghost in the Checkout Line

Okay, ladies, picture this: You just tossed some shampoo, some detergent, and a few gallons of milk into your squeaky cart at Walmart. You're trying to hurry home for dinner when, horror of all horrors, you get caught in a slow-moving checkout line. While you stand there shuffling your feet and glancing at your watch, your eyes drift to the magazine rack, and you suddenly come face-to-face with a gorgeous cover model swathed in luxurious purple satin. One glance at the woman's shiny hair, slim body, and perfect teeth, and the message hits you with all the force of a freight train: *Here's what it means to be beautiful. Here's what the world values in a woman. Here's what you use to measure your worth.* Without even realizing it, you quickly begin reviewing all your physical imperfections. A few minutes later, you walk out of Walmart feeling a little more self-conscious and a lot more insecure.

Sound familiar to anyone else?

Let's face it, being a female in the world today can be extremely frustrating, especially when it comes to the way we look. As Elder Jeffrey R. Holland pointed out in a talk given to Young Women,

> Frankly, the world has been brutal with you in this regard. You are bombarded in movies, television, fashion magazines, and advertisements with the message that looks are everything! The pitch is, "If your looks are good enough, your life will be glamorous and you

will be happy and popular." That kind of pressure is immense in the teenage years, to say nothing of later womanhood. In too many cases too much is being done to the human body to meet just such a fictional (to say nothing of superficial) standard.[1]

I'm guessing most of us would heartily agree with everything Elder Holland said, but for some reason that doesn't stop the ghostly image, the image of the "ideal woman," from continuing to haunt us. Author Lisa Bevere describes this woman with remarkable accuracy:

> She is a woman . . . adored by men and envied by women. . . .
>
> Her skin is flawless in tone and complexion. Her nose is straight—not too small or too large. Her eyes are bright and lack any dark shadows, circles, or lines around them. They are encased in luminous, wrinkle-free skin. Her lips are full and artfully shaped. Her teeth are perfect and gleaming white. Her hair is whatever ours is not.
>
> Her body is perfectly proportioned and sits atop long, strong legs. Her breasts never age (or nurse)! All too often they are not even real. She is either taller or shorter than us—the perfect height!
>
> The image is never what we are and is always just beyond our reach, taunting us with her seductive eyes. . . .
>
> Though we know she is not real, young girls and older women look at her in awe. The young are inspired, and the older are depressed.
>
> Why would someone we have never met be able to influence us so profoundly?[2]

There she is again—that purple-clad model we ran into in the checkout line. Why *does* she influence us so profoundly? Since only 4 percent of us genetically possess the ideal body as portrayed by the media,[3] you'd think we'd simply dismiss her and focus instead on just being ourselves. The trouble is, for a great majority of us, that's proven to be much easier said than done. Notice, for instance, these discouraging statistics:

- Four out of five US women are dissatisfied with their appearance.
- Two out of five women specified that they would gladly trade three to five years of their lives if they could just reach their ideal weight goals.

- In one study, three out of four women stated that they were overweight although only one out of four actually were.
- In 1970 the average age a girl started dieting was fourteen; by 1990 the average dropped to eight.
- Fifty-one percent of girls aged nine to ten stated that they felt better about themselves when they were on a diet, and one half of fourth grade girls were found to be dieting.[4]

This epidemic of body dissatisfaction hasn't just afflicted the women of the world, it's also had a huge impact on us as LDS women. Let me back up that claim with the research of Lexie and Lindsay Kite, twin sisters who have spent several years studying the representation of the female body in the media. In an insightful article in the January 2011 issue of *LDS Living* magazine, they paint this grim picture that hits way too close to home:

> Unfortunately, we as Latter-day Saints are not immune to harmful media messages. Though no religion-specific data exists to show rates of eating disorders or body image issues, numerous accounts from diligent parents, priesthood and auxiliary leaders of struggling girls, and women speak for themselves. And one of Forbes magazine's annual rankings may indicate that our quest for perfection took a wrong turn somewhere along the way: Salt Lake City, home to the worldwide headquarters of the LDS Church (and where an estimated 50 percent of the population is LDS), was ranked the "Vainest City in the Nation" in 2007 and 2008, and was in the Top 5 in 2009. This ranking is due to the city's record-breaking amount spent on beauty products and treatments like Botox, an amount that is ten-fold the amount spent in cities of comparable size. If you've looked at the billboards along any Utah freeway, you won't be shocked to hear Salt Lake City has the most plastic surgeons per capita, at six per 100,000 residents, trumping New York City and Los Angeles.[5]

Truth is, you don't need these kinds of statistics to tell you that body dissatisfaction is a common issue in our world today. How about we try a little experiment? First, think about all the women you've known over the years, like your mom, sisters, aunts, cousins, roommates, friends, and even the women in your ward. Now tell me, do you know even one woman on that list who has a healthy relationship with her body? One woman who feels completely at peace with the way she looks? It's a rare thing to find today. I'd say it's much more common to hear a friend or family member complain about how she needs to lose twenty pounds or how her hair is too flat or how her complexion just isn't what it used to be.

But let's not stop with others around us—what about *you*? Do you struggle with body image issues of your own? Is that why you picked up this book? Could you tell me everything you hate about your body from the top of your head right down to the manicured toenails sticking out of your flip-flops? If so, it just goes to show that body dissatisfaction really is a full-blown epidemic—a debilitating scourge that affects women young and old alike.

As I've pondered this particular problem, there's one nagging thought that I haven't been able to get out of my head: Those of us who've received the gospel of Jesus Christ are different from the world in that *we know who we are*. We know we're daughters of God, who have eternal significance and value in the eyes of the Lord. We know we're more than what we look like on the outside. So why have so many of us (myself included) stood in front of the mirror and winced at the image we see? Why is there such dread involved in shopping for a swimsuit—or even a pair of jeans, for that matter? Why all the inadequacy and self-condemnation? For goodness' sake, why aren't we more comfortable in our God-given skin?

With that said, the question I'm really itching to address is this: Is it even realistic for me to suggest that we should be happy and content with our physical bodies? I mean, maybe all we can hope for is some sort of half-hearted, shoulder-shrugging resignation that says, "This is the body I've got, so I better just make the best of it." I'll admit, I've been guilty of thinking exactly that. While on bad days I struggled with some pretty negative self-talk, on good days often all I could muster up was, "I guess I don't look half bad."

Well, I'm here to tell you that our Father in Heaven wants more for his daughters than that. I believe He wants us to understand not just our worth but also our true *beauty*. In fact, I believe

He wants an awareness of our own unique beauty to settle so deep into our hearts that we really, truly see ourselves the way He sees us. Just imagine how that would change your everyday life. There would be no more self-loathing or body-hatred, no more wondering what others are thinking or if they approve, and no more cringing every time you see a different number on the bathroom scale. Such a revelation would truly be groundbreaking. I believe it would free us to become what our Heavenly Father sent us to earth to become.

In fact, I'd like to suggest that it's time for us as daughters of the living God, and as "joint-heirs" with the Lord Jesus Christ Himself (Romans 8:17), to really understand who we are on the *outside* as well as the inside. It's time we learn to live in a place of joy and peace when it comes to our physical bodies. It's a goal that's very much within our reach. But before we can grasp it, there are some critical things that we women need to discuss, things that will hopefully change the way we see ourselves, our bodies, and, most important, our Savior, Jesus Christ.

To begin, sit back and relax as I tell you a very familiar and insightful little story in the next chapter.

Babylon in the 21st Century

A long time ago, on the other side of the world, three young Jews watched in shock as their worst nightmare suddenly became a reality. After thirty long months of siege against Jerusalem, a fierce Babylonian army broke through the walls of their beloved Jerusalem and began to plunder, pillage, and burn everything in sight. Once the dust settled, the trio discovered their homes reduced to rubble, Solomon's temple in enemy hands, and many religious leaders lying dead in the street. But the fate of Hananiah, Mishael, and Azariah would seem almost worse than death. Because the Babylonians valued youth who were vibrant, strong, and well-educated, soldiers clamped the three with chains and forced the young men to leave their beloved homeland and embark on a solemn march into the wild unknown.

It wasn't long before the trio found themselves standing in the court of Nebuchadnezzar, the great king of Babylon. Their instructions were simple: for the next three years, they would study the language and customs of the Chaldeans in preparation for future service to the king. To everyone's surprise, the young Jews increased so rapidly in learning and wisdom, they surpassed all others in the royal court. And when their friend Daniel successfully interpreted Nebuchadnezzar's dream, the king placed all four men in responsible positions throughout the province of Babylon. Hananiah, Mishael, and Azariah—or as the Chaldeans called them, Shadrach, Meshach, and Abed-nego—had no idea how deeply their faith would be tested in the weeks to come.

Eventually, Nebuchadnezzar hatched a plan to unite the kingdom behind his favorite form of pagan worship. As part of this plan, the king commanded his artisans to construct an enormous golden image that stood over ninety feet in the air. Roughly equivalent to a nine-story building, the monument served as the focal point for all who lived in Babylon. For the three Hebrew leaders, it was quite a staggering sight to behold.

When the day of dedication arrived, Nebuchadnezzar and his personal advisors, princes, and officers sent the following proclamation throughout the city:

> To you it is commanded, O people, nations, and languages,
>
> *That* at what time ye hear the sound of the cornet, flute, harp, sackbut, psaltery, dulcimer, and all kinds of musick, ye fall down and worship the golden image that Nebuchadnezzar the king hath set up:
>
> And whoso falleth not down and worshippeth shall the same hour be cast into the midst of a burning fiery furnace. (Daniel 3:4–6)

The minute the music began, people all across Babylon immediately prostrated themselves before the golden image. Not one Chaldean citizen remained on his feet—that is, except Shadrach, Meshach, and Abed-nego. The brave men stood firm, flatly refusing to bow before the statue in reverent worship.

Furious, Nebuchadnezzar commanded that the men be brought to him, and he again threatened them with death in a fiery furnace if they continued to disobey his orders. Undaunted, the faithful Jews replied,

> If it be *so*, our God whom we serve is able to deliver us from the burning fiery furnace, and he will deliver *us* out of thine hand, O king.
>
> But if not, be it known unto thee, O king, that we will not serve thy gods, nor worship the golden image which thou hast set up. (Daniel 3:17–18)

Now, I'm guessing you already know the end of the story. After all, it's one of the greatest triumphs ever recorded in the scriptures. Because Shadrach, Meshach, and Abed-nego refused to bow before the king's golden idol, they were thrown into a raging furnace heated seven-times hotter than usual. Miraculously, the Savior Himself showed up inside the searing furnace and wrapped the men so tightly in His protection that "the fire had no power, nor was an hair of their head singed, neither were their coats changed, nor the smell of fire had passed on them" (Daniel 3:27). It's an incredible victory that will continue to be told for generations to come.

As spectacular as that ending is, it's not the part of the story that interests us at this point. Instead, I'd like to talk a little more about that big, golden image. If you remember, in the first chapter we used the word *image* to refer to society's ideal woman. While it may seem like a stretch to compare an ancient golden statue with a purple-clad cover model, I'd like to show you some comparisons between the two. You might be surprised how well today's image of the perfect woman aligns itself with the Babylonian statue.

First, Nebuchadnezzar's statue stood so tall it could be seen from almost anywhere in Babylon. This one is easy to visualize. Just imagine what it must have been like to live in the shadow of that enormous golden image. It was probably the first thing the Chaldeans noticed when they looked out the window in the morning and the last thing they saw before going to bed at night. Even if the citizens tried to ignore the domineering statue, its penetrating stare must have seemed to follow them everywhere they went.

Now think about the town you live in and tell me, how easy is it to avoid the oppressive gaze of the ideal woman? Her face is plastered all over billboards, banners, and storefront windows. She stars in every single movie and television show we watch (and in most of the commercials as well). She smiles at us from magazines as we sit in the doctor's office, looks down at us from posters while we walk the aisles of Walmart, and sneaks up on us in those annoying pop-up ads whenever we surf the web. Just as the Babylonian image towered over every part of the Chaldean kingdom, the image of the ideal woman assaults our senses no matter where we go. As much as we try to escape her influence, she is ever-present, taunting us to bow down and worship her rail-thin body; her smooth and blemish-free skin; and her full, luxurious hair.

Second, Nebuchadnezzar's image was sculpted and molded by those who were living in Babylon. If you take a closer look at the word *image* in the scriptures, you'll find images or false gods are often described in terms of how they were created or made. For instance, in the book of Exodus, the children of Israel were told to avoid any "graven image" (Exodus 20:4), and Hosea warned of the dangers of "molten images" (Hosea 13:2). Whether these idols were formed by melting and shaping metal or by carving figures out of wood or stone, the point is that false gods in the ancient world were meticulously sculpted by talented artisans, workers who'd become masters at their particular craft.

I think we'd all agree that, in our day, the molding and sculpting of the ideal woman has reached almost ridiculous heights. Through the wonders of modern technology, a supermodel's photo is often so retouched and reworked that the finished product hardly resembles the original woman who posed for the camera. And don't forget, these doctored images are the work of master craftsmen: computer whizzes; makeup artists; and plastic surgeons who nip, tuck, and alter a model's body until her appearance takes on near-mythic proportions.

To illustrate, let me take you to a fantastic website called beautyredefined.net. It was developed by Lexie and Lindsay Kite, the twin sisters I mentioned earlier. On this site, the Kites reveal some dramatic examples of the molding and sculpting of today's ideal woman. One case they highlight comes from the September 2009 issue of *Shape* magazine where music superstar Kelly Clarkson appeared much different on the cover than she actually looked in person. When critics confronted the editor-in-chief, Lucy Danziger, about the disparity, she justified her actions with these surprising words:

> Did we alter her appearance? Only to make her look her personal best . . . But in the sense that Kelly is the picture of confidence, and she truly is, then I think this photo is the truest we have ever put out there on the newsstand.[1]

If this *Shape* editor believes that altering Ms. Clarkson's image is the only way for her to look her "personal best," what message does that send to the rest of us? As we compare ourselves with an image that isn't even real, the result will most likely be greater inadequacy and shame, since our "personal best" doesn't seem to be any more achievable than Ms. Clarkson's was. (To check out the Kites' Gallery of Photoshop Phoniness, you can search online for their article, "Photoshopping: Altering Images and Our Minds!")

You might enjoy knowing that, back in 2002, one celebrity decided she'd had enough of all this molding and sculpting. When *MORE* magazine approached Jamie Lee Curtis for an interview and photo-shoot, she told the editor she'd do so only on one condition. According to the article, "Glam Jamie [would] pose only if Real Jamie gets equal time."[2] The magazine agreed. When the piece was finally published, right next to a picture of Ms. Curtis all primped, painted, and posed was a simple shot of the actress without any makeup, hair styling, or camouflaging clothing. The comparison was striking—and brave.

So why in the world would a celebrity famous for having a perfect body willingly expose her flaws to the world? Listen to the actress's courageous answer:

> There's a reality to the way I look without my clothes on. I don't have great thighs. I have very big breasts and a soft, fatty little tummy. And I've got back fat. People assume that I'm walking around in little spaghetti-strap dresses. It's insidious—Glam Jamie, the Perfect Jamie, the great figure, blah, blah, blah. And I don't want the unsuspecting forty-year-old women of the world to think that I've got it going on. It's such a fraud. And I'm the one perpetuating it.[3]

I applaud Ms. Curtis for being bold enough to remind us that today's image of beauty is *not* based on reality. Instead, it's the work of those who try to mold, shape, and sculpt our perspective until it fits in with that of the world.

Third, the Chaldeans were given cues that caused them to fall down and worship the image. If you remember, in the scriptural story, the king used music to initiate his people's worship of the golden statue. I believe Satan also employs similar cues in our day to encourage us to bow down before the worldly image of beauty. The tricky thing is, these cues are hidden in our common, everyday experiences, so we often don't even realize that Satan is using them against us. Most of the time there's nothing wrong with the cue itself—it's how we *react to it* in our hearts and minds that causes the problem. Let me give you a few examples and you'll see the image worship that can be triggered by these deceptive little cues:

- Cue: We watch a movie with our husband and he mentions that the actress is really attractive.
  Reaction: His words make us feel dowdy, plain, and ugly, and we begin to think about different ways we can copy her look.
- Cue: We're having a bad hair day and a friend walks into church with a hairstyle that looks like it came right out of a magazine.
  Reaction: We shrink a little in our seat and try to figure out if we have time to go home and redo our hair.
- Cue: Standing in the checkout line, we see tabloid pictures that shame various celebrities for having cellulite.
  Reaction: We instantly feel shame for having our own cellulite and we ponder starting yet another diet.
- Cue: An entire section of our Pinterest board is dedicated to fashion.
  Reaction: As we browse through our favorite pins, we begin to feel dissatisfied with our wardrobe and we become obsessed with finding clothes that make us look more like the women in the pictures.
- Cue: A friend starts talking about a new skin care product that has made a huge difference in the tiny lines and wrinkles on her face.
  Reaction: We immediately run to the store and buy that very same product for ourselves.

These are just a few drops in the giant sea of cues that washes over us every single day of our lives. How do we recognize these cues? It's easy. In short, a cue is anything that causes us to obsess about the image, anything that makes us yearn to fit our body and appearance to the standard of the world. Satan calls to us just like Nebuchadnezzar's flutes and cornets—only in this case he uses persuasive language, attractive pictures, and alluring statistics. Subtly he promises us that, if we'll just dedicate ourselves to pursuing the image, all our dreams will finally come true. But all these cues really do is invite us to give ourselves over to idolatry, to bow ourselves down before the golden image of the world.

Fourth, the Chaldeans were warned that if they didn't worship the image, they would die. At first glance, this comparison doesn't seem to apply to our generation, does it? We're not threatened with death if we never achieve flat abs or get down to a size two. Or are we? I'd like to suggest that death threats weren't just a Babylonian tactic; they're also used against us in our day and age.

Let me introduce you to an author who started out on a journey to explore the topic of obesity, but who ultimately discovered a very different story than the one the media has been telling us for decades. In *The Obesity Myth: Why America's Obsession with Weight Is Hazardous to Your Health*, author Paul Campos reveals this astounding conclusion:

> [After] plowing through dozens of books, hundreds of articles in medical journals, and countless interviews with medical and scientific experts, I discovered that almost everything the government and the media were saying about weight and weight control was either grossly distorted or flatly untrue. . . .
>
> The medical and public health establishment has . . . done so by systematically distorting the available evidence regarding the relationship between weight and health, [and] by severely exaggerating the risks [of being overweight]. . . .
>
> Never before in American history has so much junk science been exploited to whip up hysteria about a supposed public health "epidemic."[4]

Campos then backs up his claim with some pretty compelling evidence. For example, one study he cites followed six hundred thousand subjects for up to thirty years and found that a non-smoking woman of average height could weigh anywhere within an eighty pound range without seeing any increased risk of an early death.[5] Another study followed thousands of men in seven different nations for forty years and discovered that the thinnest men were the ones who died the earliest.[6] Campos also uncovered several studies in medical journals proving that even massively obese men and women aren't more prone to heart disease than usual.[7] And he found at least nine studies confirming that the heavier a person is, the less chance they have of dying of cancer.[8] In the end, Campos was shocked to learn that the majority of the epidemiological evidence suggests that *it's more hazardous to be five pounds underweight than to be seventy-five pounds overweight.*[9]

Now, whether or not you buy Campos's argument isn't the issue. The issue we need to grapple with is this: Why doesn't the media ever tell us about these kinds of studies? Until reading Campos's book, I'd never heard anything of the sort. I believed what the news reports told me again and again: if I wasn't thin like the image, if my BMI didn't fall within government recommended standards, I was more likely to die an early death. Why not tell us the truth? I believe the answer lies in the very next comparison.

Fifth, Nebuchadnezzar's image was made of gold, meaning it was worth a great deal of money. In his book *Fat Politics: The Real Story behind America's Obesity Epidemic* (which reports many of the same conclusions as *The Obesity Myth*), author J. Eric Oliver makes this point:

> Over the past two decades, a handful of scientists, doctors, and health officials have actively campaigned to define our growing weight as an "obesity epidemic." They have created a very low and arbitrary definition of what is "overweight" and "obese" so that tens of millions of Americans, including archetypes of fitness such as President George Bush or basketball star Michael Jordan, are now considered to "weigh too much." They have also inflated the dangers and distorted the statistics about weight and health, exaggerated the impact of obesity on everything from motor accidents to air pollution. And, most important, they have established body weight as a barometer of wellness, so that being thin is equated with being healthy.[10]

Oliver then offers his reason for this gross exaggeration of reality. He says it's motivated by one thing—money.

Consider, for example, what an obesity epidemic means for the following groups. For scientists researching issues of weight, an obesity epidemic inflates their stature and allows them to get more research grants. For government health agencies, it is a powerful rationale for increasing their programs and budget allocations. For weight-loss companies and surgeons, it is a way to get their services covered by Medicare and health insurance providers. And, for pharmaceutical companies it can justify the release of new drugs, and help inflate their stock prices. The very same people who have proclaimed that obesity is a major health problem also stand the most to gain from it being classified as a disease. For America's public health establishment, an obesity epidemic is worth billions.[11]

To add even more fuel to the fire, take a gander at this list of moneymakers highlighted by Eric A. Finkelstein and Laurie Zuckerman in their book, *The Fattening of America*:

> The weight-loss industry is a $49 billion per year industry. Diet centers and programs; diet camps; prepackaged foods; over-the-counter diet drugs; diet patches; fat blockers; starch blockers; magnet pills; bulk producers; algae, weight-loss books and magazines; electrical muscle stimulators; nutritionists; commercial and residential exercise clubs; sugar-free, fat-free, and reduced calorie food products; and imitation fats and sugar substitutes are everywhere, and they are increasingly profitable.[12]

Of course, our weight issues aren't the only way money-grabbers are exploiting our attachment to the image. Corporations also rake in huge profits on things like fashion magazines, beauty products, and famous label clothing. In other words, take away the image and there would be a whole a lot of millionaires out of work. It all comes down to the fact that the more the world worships the image, the more vendors' pockets will be filled with the thing they love the most: money.

Those five comparisons are intriguing, don't you think? These comparisons opened my eyes to the truth lurking beneath the surface of our current beauty culture—the truth that the image of the ideal woman isn't simply a dangerous distraction or an unrealistic goal. Instead, it's a false god, a big golden idol, a graven image that's been formed and created by the hands of the world. And that means it's something that we Latter-day Saints must avoid like the plague. Like Shadrach, Meshach, and Abed-nego, we too must turn from this idol with all our heart, might, mind, and strength.

With that said, I have to admit that this is the point where the story breaks down for me. You see, I can't in good conscience compare myself to the three faithful Hebrews. Though I wish things were different, the truth is that rather than shunning this particular idol, for the past twenty-five years I've been a card-carrying, dyed-in-the-wool image worshipper. In other words, I bought the idea, hook, line, and sinker. I bowed down before the image, devoted myself to it, and did everything I could to make it my own.

But before you judge me too harshly, let me say in my defense that those who know me might be a little confused by my confession. After all, I've never been one to pour over glamour magazines or spend every spare minute at the mall. Friends would more likely run into me in a thrift store than a trendy new boutique. No, I'm not into designer labels, I don't follow the fashion industry, and I've never tried to copy a famous celebrity's appearance. In the end, I'm just a regular mom whose clothes more often sport peanut-butter smudges or the faint smell of 409.

So why would I label myself an image worshipper? Because I devoted myself to the image in more subtle ways that hid themselves under the guise of my daily life. I'll explain what I mean by that eventually, but for now, my point is that the Lord finally called me on my idolatry. Big time. Though I never labeled my thoughts and actions as "worship," He certainly did. In fact, He unveiled image worship in me that was so blatant and intentional, it left me stunned. This revelation opened my eyes so dramatically, I've never been able to look at physical beauty the same way again.

For example, while I was studying the concept of *worship*, I discovered that the word itself means "to be devoted to."[13] At that moment, I couldn't deny that I'd spent many years "devoted to" the pursuit of a thinner, more beautiful me. Though I would probably have said my efforts were centered on "getting healthier," underneath that rationalization, what I really wanted was to mold myself to better fit the image, to be considered beautiful in the eyes of the world.

If nothing else, what I hope my confession reveals is that our personal worship isn't as cut-and-dried as we may think. Our idolatry can manifest itself not only in our outward behavior but also in simple things like a thought, a feeling, or an intent of the heart. Our enemy knows that if he can just get us to devote ourselves, in even the smallest ways, to the worldly image of beauty, we'll be caught in sin of idolatry. Though we may not even recognize it, we'll be worshipping a very deceitful but very powerful false god. For this reason, I'd like you to join me as we explore the world of an image worshipper. It's a dynamic that's extremely easy to get tangled up in. But make no mistake, it's also a world that the daughters of Zion must leave behind once and for all.

For Additional Study

Grab your scriptures and turn to 1 John 2:15. How do you think this verse applies to our discussion of the golden image? In what ways have you personally manifested a love for the things of the world, especially things that promise to make you more thin or beautiful?

Next, look up Isaiah 41:29. Let's relate the prophet's words to our society's standard of beauty. How do you think today's image is "vanity"? Why is it "nothing" in the eyes of the Lord? Also, ponder how the image could be considered "wind and confusion."

In 3 Nephi 21:14–17, what do we learn about the eventual fate of all graven images? How do you think that applies to the beauty culture that exists in our world today?

What is the consequence specified in Deuteronomy 8:19 for those who choose to worship false gods? See also Ezekiel 5:11. How could these verses apply to you personally?

Take a minute to evaluate your own relationship with the image. What cues seem to work best on you? Is there a particular characteristic of the image that appeals to you most? How often do you mentally compare yourself with the standard of the world? (We'll discuss this idea in greater depth in the next chapter.)

A Portrait of an Image Worshipper

As we begin our examination of an image worshipper, we face a really tricky situation. You see, in Nebuchadnezzar's day it was easy to spot those devoted to the image since they were the ones planting their faces to the floor. But we all know it doesn't work that way anymore. Chances are you'll never see a woman kneeling in awe before a Victoria's Secret catalog or bowing down to a pair of patent leather pumps she happened to find on sale. So how do we measure idolatry in our generation? What does it look like in the small moments of our everyday lives?

One way to answer that question is by looking at a characteristic common to all worshippers: *sacrifice*. Remember, the image of beauty is a false god that demands sacrifice just like the true and living God. So it follows that those who choose to worship this particular idol will sacrifice a great deal in the name of physical attractiveness. To illustrate, I'd like to highlight some of the most common offerings laid on the altar by image worshippers. Unfortunately, I've been guilty of almost everything on the following list. I'm guessing a few of these sacrifices will sound familiar to you as well.

An image worshipper sacrifices her time, money, and energy in devotion to the image. When it comes to sacrifice, most of us probably think first of all the time, money, and energy we give to our family, our church, and our community. While I'd never want to minimize those important contributions, I think it's time for each of us to take a good hard look at what we're doing with all the time, money, and energy that isn't being devoted to those noble causes.

For instance, in our spare time, are we spending hours fussing over our hair or combing the mall for the right clothes? Are we blowing our money on the latest weight loss drug or that new anti-aging cream? Are we exhausting our energy maintaining an intense exercise program or counting every calorie we put into our mouth? If so, it just goes to show that an image worshipper is certainly willing to sacrifice.

I have to admit that when I took a closer look at my own daily routine, I realized that, even though I offered a great deal of service to both my family and the Lord, I was also devoting countless hours, hundreds of dollars, and a mountain of energy in an attempt to make myself thinner and more beautiful. Though I never bowed before a golden statue, all the time, money, and energy I was dedicating to my appearance revealed my heart's true devotion. Like the idolaters Hosea spoke of, my "heart [was] divided;" part of me dearly loved the Lord and His work, but part of me was also busy chasing the golden image of the world (Hosea 10:2).

An image worshipper sacrifices her thoughts to the pursuit of the image. Maybe we're not even aware that we're doing it. Maybe it doesn't seem like that big of a deal. Still, it's important to ask ourselves how often our mind is focused on our personal body image. It may be that we mull over which diet to try next or which makeup tricks will minimize our flaws. Or perhaps we're caught up in thoughts of self-condemnation and body-hatred. Even simple ideas like "I don't have anything decent to wear" or "I've got to get my weight under control" can so overtake our thoughts that we're unable to focus on anything but the power of the image. As a result, our mind spins in a debilitating cycle of guilt, shame, or all-out hopelessness.

In contrast, the gospel of Jesus Christ sets a much different standard when it comes to our mind. For example, the Lord tells us to "look unto [Him] in every thought," and to make our "minds . . . single to God" (D&C 6:36, 88:68). I had to admit that this just wasn't my reality. Instead, a huge portion of my thought life was devoted to how I looked in the mirror or, on other days, how I just wasn't good enough. Though I tried to deny my tendency to obsess, I couldn't hide it from the Lord. He knew perfectly the "thoughts and the intents of [my] heart" (D&C 6:16), and that, behind my outwardly religious façade, my mind revealed the mental devotion of an image worshipper.

An image worshipper sacrifices her healthy metabolism when she turns to dieting to help her look like the image. Women devoted to the image know well the language and culture of the dieter. How else will we squeeze ourselves into those skinny jeans calling to us from the back of our closet? As we vigorously study the habits of successful dieters, we do all we can to adopt those same strategies as our own. Yet most of the time, we watch helplessly as our weight yo-yos down for a while, then right back up again. Frustrated, we muster up more willpower in the hopes that we'll discover the diet plan or exercise routine that will finally help us hit the jackpot. Authors Evelyn Tribole and Elyse Resch describe the scenario this way:

> "Please, please, let the number be . . ." This wishful number prayer is not occurring in the casinos of Las Vegas, but in private homes throughout the country. But just like the desperate gambler waiting for his lucky number to come in, so is it futile for the dieter to pay homage to the "scale god.'" In one sweep of the scale roulette, hopes and desperation create a daily drama that will ultimately shape what mood you'll be in for the day.[1]

I think it's telling that these nutritionists refer to the scale not only as a "scale god" but also a "false idol."[2]

I'll confess that I can hardly remember a time when I wasn't on some kind of diet, or at least thinking about starting one. It all began when puberty left my body a natural size twelve, a size my young, image-saturated mind couldn't accept as final. As a result, my life quickly turned into a long string of on-again, off-again diets. The crazy thing is, no matter how many times a diet failed, I still believed deep in my heart that next time I'd find "the one" that would make me a perpetual size six. In the end, though, all that thinking did was saddle me with feelings of discouragement, insecurity, and frustration.

Of course, research has now revealed what we dieters have long suspected: diets don't work. Not only that, but they mess with our body's chemistry in such a way that, after dieting, we're left worse off than if we'd never dieted at all. As nutritionist Debra Waterhouse points out:

> If women knew what dieting really does to their bodies, they would never, ever even think about the new diet they plan to start on Monday. As soon as your fat cells realize that calories have been reduced, they throw a party and invite the lipogenic enzymes to store fat. Unfortunately, lipolytic [or fat-releasing] enzymes are not on the guest list. Dieting simply increases the size of your fat cells, improves your body's ability to store fat, and limits your ability to burn it. . . .
>
> If you want to store more fat . . .
> If you want larger fat cells . . .
> If you want more fat cells . . .
> If you want less muscle mass . . .
> If you want a slower metabolism . . .
> If you want to gain weight . . .
> . . . . GO ON A DIET. [3]

The conclusion that dieting boosts our fat-storing enzymes is also mentioned by Tribole and Resch who add that chronic dieting also results in increased binge eating, preoccupation with food, feelings of deprivation, and a sense of failure. [4] In addition, they highlight the vicious "diet backlash effect," which is "characterized by periods of careful eating, 'blowing it,' and paying penance with more dieting or extra-careful eating." [5] It's a cycle that repeats itself over and over and over in the life of a dieter.

To those of us stuck in this never-ending cycle, author Paul Campos asks this haunting question: "Are fifty or sixty years of slavery to the false gods of slenderness . . . worth the reward that may come from spending ten or twenty thousand days in bondage to the food diary and the calorie counter?" [6] His point should cause each of us to ask ourselves: Am I a slave to the false god of slenderness? And more important, do I really want to spend the rest of my life stuck in this miserable type of bondage?

An image worshipper sacrifices a natural and easy relationship with food in order to better resemble the image. In light of what we just discussed about dieting, I want you to read through the following verses with a fresh pair of eyes:

> Verily I say, . . . the fulness of the earth is yours, the beasts of the field and the fowls of the air, and that which climbeth upon the trees and walketh upon the earth;
>
> Yea, and the herb, and the good things which come of the earth, whether for food or for raiment, or for houses, or for barns, or for orchards, or for gardens, or for vineyards;
>
> Yea, all things which come of the earth, in the season thereof, are made for the benefit and the use of man, both to please the eye and to gladden the heart;
>
> Yea, for food and for raiment, for taste and for smell, to strengthen the body and to enliven the soul (D&C 59:16–19).

What the Lord is saying in this passage is that food was actually meant to bring us joy, to "gladden [our] heart" and "enliven [our] soul." But rather than enjoying the blessings of food, image worshippers learn to eat in very unnatural ways.

Tribole and Resch have names for these kinds of eaters. The Careful Eater scrutinizes every bite of food taken into her body, meticulously counting every calorie and planning every meal. The Professional Dieter is always on some kind of joy-stealing, guilt-inducing diet. The Chaotic Unconscious Eater grabs whatever she can on the run, without much thought to nutrition or even tasting her food. And the Emotional Unconscious Eater "range[s] from grabbing a candy bar in stressful times to chronic compulsive binges of vast quantities of food."[7] Needless to say, the Doctrine and Covenants reveals that this is not how the Lord intended us to eat or to live.

One of my wake-up call moments came through the words of nutritionist Michelle May, who helped me realize the many ways I'd lost the joy of food and eating. She asks,

> Do you feel guilty when you eat certain foods? . . . Are you confused about what you're supposed to eat? Do you obsess about everything you eat? When you eat something you think you shouldn't, is it hard to stop? . . .

Do you say you love to eat but eat so fast that you barely notice the taste after the first few bites? . . .

Do you eat because you're hungry? Do you even know what hunger feels like anymore? Do you eat because it's time to, because the food looks good, or because you're stressed, bored, or one of a thousand other reasons? Does eating make you feel better—but only for a little while? Does that sometimes lead to even more eating? . . .

Have you forgotten that the purpose of eating is to fuel your life?"[8]

If, like me, you answered yes to most of her questions, tell me: Do you ever wonder what your life would be like if you'd never allowed the marketers of the image to change your relationship with food? Can you even imagine a world without dieting, a world where a meal simply serves to strengthen your body and gladden your heart? Perhaps it's time for us to return eating to the place where God intended it to be. Perhaps it's time to shatter the dieting idol once and for all.

An image worshipper sacrifices the joy of bearing children, since pregnancy and childbirth cause side effects that mar the perfection of the image. I don't think it's a coincidence that having flat abs is one of today's most coveted beauty features. After all, that's the first thing to go once a woman becomes pregnant—and Satan knows it. For this reason, I believe he took special care to make sure the golden image of beauty included the one thing most women lose in childbearing. Of course, the same goes with changes in our breasts, hips, and thighs as well. To the world, a post-baby body is a shameful body, as evidenced by books like *Get Your Body Back* or *Lose Your Mummy Tummy*. Even if an image worshipper values pregnancy and having children, the voices of the world often make her desperate to reverse (or at least hide) the effects of that childbearing process.

I'll admit that I didn't have a six-pack even before I had children. And after seven pregnancies, after watching my abdomen blow up like a balloon again and again, I'm certainly no closer to sporting that feature than I was before. But I will say that having children made me much more conscious of my body's supposed flaws, especially my not-so-flat stomach. I can't tell you how many times I've sucked in my belly in public, or even in front of my husband. Thankfully other parts of my body couldn't be sucked in or I'd probably have passed out from oxygen deprivation. In the end, this behavior revealed more than just my stupidity—it marked me as a true image worshipper. Rather than focusing on the beautiful thing my body had accomplished, I spent my time criticizing my outward appearance and trying to dress in a way that concealed my enormous sense of shame.

An image worshipper sacrifices her personal uniqueness and individuality in favor of the image. It's no secret that we women have been created in every shape and size imaginable: tall and lean, short and curvy, or somewhere in between. However, the world's image of beauty makes no allowance for such diversity. Instead, the message is crammed down our throats that we must all be the same size—*extremely thin*. As a result, an image worshipper desperately tries to fit herself to a mold that may not even be genetically realistic for her natural size and shape. She's not able to rejoice in her own distinct beauty because she's too caught up in trying to be someone she's not.

As for me, I'd always dreamt of changing three of my body's features: I wanted a smaller backside, a tighter tummy, and thick, luxurious hair. Never mind that none of these things came naturally to me. No, for some reason I believed that if I just focused on these particular features, I could eventually find a way to change the way I looked. One day, I came across the following counsel from Sister Patricia T. Holland in her insightful book, *A Quiet Heart*:

> It is as the Savior himself told his disciples: "Take no thought for your life, what ye shall eat, or what ye shall drink; nor yet for your body, what ye shall put on" (Matthew 6:25). He told them not to worry about "things," about so much that is so temporal— you know, what am I going to wear and I hope they notice my nails. . . ."Is not the life more than meat, and the body more than raiment?" he asked. In almost these terms he said, "You are silly to spend so much time worrying about temporal and often petty things because you can't do very much about them anyway." Now, that is my loose translation of what he said. What he *really* said was,

"Which of you by taking thought [or by worrying about it] can add one cubit unto his [or her] stature?" (Matthew 6:27). Why waste time worrying that we are 4'11" and, well, "solid" when we would like to be 5'9" and slinky? These are the wrong concerns about the wrong things because they are things we can't change.[9]

While her words certainly resonated with me, it was still hard to stop obsessing over the parts of my body that I hated. Thankfully, we'll talk later about how we can overcome those consuming thoughts and feelings once and for all.

For the moment, though, I want you to consider this one important question: Now that we've worked our way through the sacrifices of an image worshipper, did you notice any of this same behavior in your own life? Remember, the list of sacrifices we just covered is not exhaustive. Sacrifice always begins with thoughts of devotion, so it's time for you to ask yourself how you've worshipped the image through your devoted thoughts or sacrificial actions. Personally, it was sobering for me to realize that when the Lord said, "Every man walketh . . . after the image of his own god, whose image is in the likeness of the world" (D&C 1:16), He was actually talking about me. In short, I worshipped the image every time I thought more about fat grams than His gospel, every time I spent more time on my hair and makeup than on prayer and scriptures, and every time I admired those who modeled the worldly image rather than the true "image of God" (Alma 5:19).

Elder David A. Bednar summed up my situation with these insightful words: "When any of Heavenly Father's children misuse their physical tabernacles by . . . worshipping the false idol of body image, whether their own or that of others, Satan is delighted."[10] He then offered the following counsel:

> I cannot tell you all the ways whereby you may misuse your bodies, "for there are divers ways and means, even so many that I cannot number them" (Mosiah 4:29). You know what is right and what is wrong, and you have the individual responsibility to learn for yourself "by study and also by faith" (D&C 88:118). . . . I testify that as you desire to so learn, as you "watch yourselves, and your thoughts, and your words, and your deeds, and observe the commandments of God, and continue in the faith of what ye have

heard concerning the coming of our Lord, even unto the end of your lives" (Mosiah 4:30), you will be spiritually enlightened and protected. And according to your faithfulness and diligence, you will have the power to discern the deception and repel the attacks of the adversary as he tempts you to misuse your physical body.[11]

To follow Elder Bednar's direction, I'd like you to join me as we address some additional principles associated with image worship. One of the most important things we need to deal with is why the image is so appealing to us in the first place. As I pondered this particular question, the Spirit revealed a number of reasons why the world's standard of beauty was so attractive to me. To my surprise, this sparked a chain reaction that, for the first time in my life, broke the power of the image in my mind and heart.

As a result, I now believe that the only way we can turn from our image worship is to do what Elder Bednar said: to learn for ourselves by study and by faith how the Lord views both our body and our beauty. Only then will we have the power "to discern the deception and repel the attacks of the adversary." Only then will we be "spiritually enlightened and protected" against this dangerous and influential assault on the daughters of God.

For Additional Study

Take a minute to add up the time you spend every day on activities that promote your physical beauty. This includes doing hair and makeup, shopping for clothes, managing your diet, doing your nails, reading about something body-related, etc. How much time do you spend on such activities?

Now take a day or two to track what percentage of your time is spent *thinking about* your outward appearance. This includes anything from obsessing over your flaws to thinking about losing weight to fantasizing about the body you wish you had. How often are you caught up in these kinds of thoughts? What do you think that reveals about your personal worship?

Turn to Mormon 8:35–39. After reading this passage, take a second look at verse 39. Do your body image concerns ever consume you to the point where you're unaware of the needs or feelings of others? What else do these verses teach us about becoming pre-occupied with the worldly image of beauty?

In the Old Testament, Jehovah makes His feelings about image worship very clear in 1 Kings 14:9. How do you think this verse could apply to your own life?

With regard to your weight, how much have you sacrificed in an attempt to make yourself thinner? For instance, are you mired in a cycle of yo-yo dieting? Do you binge and purge? Do you force yourself to remain on a severely restricted diet? If you answered yes to any of these questions, have you ever thought about *why* you practice these behaviors? When did it all start? What is the root cause of your unhealthy relationship with food?

If you've given birth, how did you respond to the physical changes that came as a result of your pregnancy? Did the child-bearing process increase your sense of shame? Do you feel your pregnancy robbed you of your beauty? If so, why do you think that is?

Read through Moses chapter 1 in the Pearl of Great Price. The word *worship* actually appears several times in this chapter. As you study Moses's encounter with God and also with Satan, evaluate what his experience teaches us about who we choose to worship, and especially how we overcome the temptation to worship any type of false god.

Turning Glory into Shame

Recently I came across a blog that really rattled me. This particular blog contained the musings of a Christian writer, speaker, and mother named Nicole Unice who was trying to decide what to give up for Lent. In case you've never heard of Lent before, it's a Christian period of fasting and preparation that begins on Ash Wednesday and culminates forty days later on Easter Sunday. It's a time when many Christians fast from a favorite food or activity in order to draw closer to God. To my surprise, Nicole revealed that she received an "unmistakable impression" that she should "give up makeup for Lent."

Here's how Nicole explains it:

> At first I thought I was mistaken, that couldn't possibly be what I was hearing. I mean, who gives up *makeup* for Lent? I love makeup. It's no big deal, it makes me feel good and bright and ready for the day! I have six speaking engagements over Lent! I can't not wear makeup and stand in front of people! Plus, God, did I mention I like it?
>
> Sound ridiculous? Yep. And that exact monologue is the exact reason why this is a good idea.
>
> There's nothing wrong with makeup, and I plan to go immediately back to it on Resurrection Sunday. But, like many other good things in my life, I am prone to making luxuries necessities. Makeup is fun. But sometimes it makes me hide. Sometimes it helps me be more of my false self, less of my ideal self. It's vanity.

Today I head out for a full day of work. I feel stripped, another reason I know this is a good decision. I take the extra ten minutes in the morning to read a Lenten devotion. I feel those feelings of insecurity rise up and instead of pressing them back I let them go, up and away, rising to my God who is incredibly creative and intimately involved in shaping me into his exact impression of beauty. And I believe that has very little to do with my eyeliner.

So I submit to this one small sacrifice, to the extra minutes each morning to remember the great and wondrous and crazy God I serve, one who uses bread from the sky and talking donkeys and bronze snakes and palm trees and mustard seeds to teach us about Himself. And I'm smiling.

Why not makeup?[1]

My first impression after reading her blog was, "Whew. I'm glad I've never received such a prompting. No makeup for six speaking engagements? I don't think I could do it." Then I thought, "Oh, no. Maybe that's why I stumbled across this blog . . . because the Lord wants me to experience the same thing for myself!" I won't minimize the panic that consumed me at that moment. I mean, why couldn't He ask me to make dinner for the neighbors or help clean the church? I'd do that ten times over before giving up makeup. With those fearful thoughts stirring around in my head, the Lord's voice penetrated my heart with more force than a loudspeaker at a football game: *Jaci, I didn't have you read the blog so you'd copy her experience. I had you read it so you could see how attached you are to this one simple thing.*

Talk about an eye-opening revelation. I sat there for a few minutes, completely taken aback. Eventually, I began to wonder why I felt such a strong aversion to the thought of going without makeup. It took some soul-searching and self-evaluation, but I finally uncovered the real issue hiding behind my fear. I knew it wasn't going without mascara or eyeliner that bothered me, since I'd occasionally shopped, driven carpool, and entertained visiting teachers without putting any on. No, the thing I couldn't live without was my concealer.

You know that woman with the beautiful complexion whose skin resembles fine porcelain? Well, let's just say that's never been me. Instead, I've endured mild acne for most of my life. And in my thirties and forties, I've developed hormone-related cysts that take a long time to clear up, even if I see a specialist for an injection. So you can understand why I reach for my concealer every time I leave the house. Without it, I truly feel naked or stripped, just like Nicole Unice said.

It's an interesting word, isn't it? *Concealer.* According to the dictionary, it means "to hide; [to] withdraw or remove from observation; [or to] cover or keep from sight."[2] It reminds me of Adam and Eve covering themselves with aprons in the Garden of Eden. I can just picture them hurriedly gathering the largest fig leaves and stringing them together into one big piece. I bet it was comforting to have a way to cover their nakedness so they would no longer feel awkward or insecure. In fact, we know the couple went even further and "hid themselves . . . amongst the trees of the garden" (Genesis 3:8). In other words, they carefully concealed their bodies so their vulnerability couldn't be exposed in any way.

And yet, let's not forget that they weren't always worried about concealing themselves like that in the Garden of Eden. The scriptures reveal that in the beginning, Adam and Eve "were . . . naked . . . *and were not ashamed*" (Genesis 2:25). Notice that it was only *after* the couple tasted the bitter fruit that they felt their first stirrings of shame, and it was only *after* they tangled with the serpent that they felt the need to grab some aprons and go into hiding.

I'd like to suggest that the same thing happened to each of us as we transitioned from childhood to womanhood. Just like Adam and Eve, we started out completely at peace with our physical body. As toddlers, we ran around naked without any reservation, rejoicing in our body's ability to taste, touch, smell, feel, and wiggle. As young girls, we looked in the mirror and saw a stunning princess who would dazzle the heart of any suitor. But as we got older, we took our first few bites of the bitter fruit—we began to internalize the world's ideas about what a physical body should look like. Only when we started to compare ourselves with the golden image of beauty did we see our hair as too thin and our hips as too wide; only then did we feel the need to cover and hide our body's imperfections.

I want you to take a minute to think about how your life follows this basic scriptural pattern. You may not use concealer as a fig leaf like I do, but I bet you have other ways you hide your insecurities about your physical body. For instance, do you try to disguise your love handles, your small breasts, or your varicose veins? Do you cover your freckles, your gray hair, or your skimpy eyelashes? Do you turn off the light when you're getting undressed or refuse to answer the door when you're in your jammies? No matter what type of fig leaves you choose, I'd say most of us react to our physical bodies just like Adam and Eve.

If it will help, I'll share a time several years ago when I desperately wanted to cover my body and hide in shame. It happened in college when some friends invited me to join them on a group date. The plans for the evening included something I absolutely loved: swimming. I'd spent my childhood in Florida and took to water like a fish, so the prospect of leaving the Idaho cold behind and diving into a cool, refreshing pool sounded like the perfect date-night activity.

The problem was, as I prepared for the date, all I could think about was how the other girls were much more well-endowed and slim-hipped than I was. It didn't help that once we arrived at the pool, I could clearly see they filled out their swimsuits in all the right places. Want to guess what I spent the whole night doing? That's right—obsessing over how awful I looked in my swimsuit. The thought so overwhelmed and embarrassed me that I didn't enjoy swimming at all. Instead, I counted the minutes until I could return to the locker room and cover myself with as many layers of fig leaves as possible.

Years later, I found a verse in Psalms that perfectly describes my behavior on that painful night: "O ye [daughters] of men, how long will ye turn my glory into shame?" (Psalm 4:2). Isn't that exactly what I'd been doing on my date? I'd taken the glorious gift of a physical body—one that could walk and talk and run and jump and swim—and turned it into shame. That night I was humiliated and ashamed, not because my body looked as frightening as I thought it did, but because I was comparing myself to the worldly image of beauty. Just like those in Lehi's dream who partook of the fruit and then "cast their eyes about as if they were ashamed," I too dismissed the gift I'd been given because my mind conjured up the mocking voices of those in the great and spacious building (1 Nephi 8:25).

Unfortunately, that's only one of the thousands of times I turned my glory into shame by measuring my body against the unforgiving standard of the world. Again and again, I ignored the blessings of having a physical body and focused instead on what I saw as its many flaws and failings. All I got for my efforts was greater embarrassment and insecurity every time I looked in the mirror.

This frustrating cycle has made me think a lot about Adam and Eve, especially how it was the Fall that seemed to trigger their feelings of shame. I've wondered, what was it about becoming mortal that caused such anxiety for the couple? As I pondered that particular question, the Spirit led me back to the very beginning—to the time before any of us were even born.

Come with me as we part the veil and return to the splendor of the premortal world. As we do so, imagine what it must have been like to live as spirit children of heavenly parents. Picture what it may have felt like to gaze on the beauty of their resurrected bodies. I'm sure the sight lit within us a burning desire to obtain a radiant, exalted body for ourselves. Thankfully, our Father in Heaven instituted the plan of salvation, which allowed us to come to earth and obtain the physical bodies we'd so fervently been longing for.

But let's not forget that, because of the consequences of the Fall, we were born into this world with *mortal* bodies, not *immortal* ones. And as we all know, mortal bodies come with some very unpleasant side-effects. We get warts, ingrown toenails, and cellulite. We endure cold sores, acne, and bad breath. On top of that, our bodies grow old and deteriorate; we suffer various diseases and disabilities. And we're subject to physical injuries that can scar us for the rest of our lives. With all these imperfections and maladies to deal with, it's easy to see why we at times feel ashamed just like Adam and Eve did when their bodies became mortal.

So maybe the real issue isn't our shame, since that's to be expected as a result of the Fall. Maybe the real issue is how we choose to deal with these feelings when they arise. Obviously, we can listen to voices of the world that tell us to cover our insecurities with makeup or hair dye or anti-aging cream—or designer jeans or body shapers or plastic surgery. If we choose to take that path, though, we'll quickly discover that those things are just a lousy bunch of fig leaves, since their flimsy covering offers us no protection against future attacks of worthlessness or shame.

In the end, what we need most isn't fancier fig leaves or better places to hide. What we need most is the same thing Adam and Eve needed: a Savior who can call us out of hiding, dismantle our clumsily sewn aprons, and heal our debilitating sense of shame. Don't forget, that's the very thing the Lord did for the couple in the Garden of Eden. In fact, once He clothed Adam and Eve in "coats of skins" of His own making (Genesis 3:21), we never hear another word about them sewing fig-leaf aprons or running off to hide in shame.

If you'll stay with me, I promise we'll learn how Christ can clothe each of us in such a way that our insecurity and shame disappears once and for all. But for now, we need to continue to work our way through the body image issues that are clogging our hearts, distracting our minds, and entangling our lives. Only as we truly understand the extent of the problem can we prepare ourselves for the Lord's miraculous cure.

For Additional Study

In your mind, what physical characteristics do you use to determine true beauty? Why do you think you've chosen that particular criteria? One way to answer that would be to think of a woman you believe is beautiful. What do you admire about her appearance? Could it be that you admire her because her body resembles the golden image of the world?

If you were to place your body image somewhere on the following spectrum, where do you think it would fall?

Obsession—Confidence—Acceptance—Resignation—Inadequacy—Shame—Hatred

How do you think the Lord would respond to a woman who feels shame or hatred for her God-given body? The following scriptures provide a few added insights about the eternal nature of our body: Psalms 139:13–16, Doctrine and Covenants 88:15, and Doctrine and Covenants 138:17.

When it comes to feelings of hatred for our body, read Jeremiah 30:8–22 and consider the following questions:

- Do you believe the "sorrow" you feel over your body is "incurable"? (verse 15 footnote).
- What does the Lord have to say about that in the *JST* footnote of verse 12?
- What does He promise to do in verse 8?
- How about in verses 10–11?
- What could be the "healing medicines" Christ uses to heal your negative body image (verse 12a)?

Dressing for the Eyes of Others

Just in case the last chapter left you wondering if you should throw your mascara out the window, I want to be very clear that there's a positive side to the whole makeup thing. Yes, at times we use it to cover up our imperfections or to disguise the effects of the Fall, but wouldn't you agree that, for women young and old alike, putting on makeup and dressing up can be just plain *fun*? Think about it for a minute. As a little girl, didn't you love clomping around the house in your mom's high heels or smearing her lipstick all over your face? Didn't you squeal over a trunk filled with sequins, feather boas, and ballerina tutus? In our family, even my tomboy daughter, who wouldn't be caught dead in pink, still rifled through our dress-up box on a regular basis. It's almost as if we females are genetically programmed to love adorning ourselves with beautiful things.

Two of my married nieces reinforced this idea recently as we talked about the habits of their young daughters. I loved hearing how one eighteen-month-old insisted on wearing her play necklaces from the moment she woke up until the minute her mother tucked her into bed at night. And her cousin hauled her purse and fancy pink shoes with her everywhere she went. I laughed as both moms assured me that they'd never encouraged their daughters to do these things. It just seemed to come naturally.

Of course, this love for pretty things doesn't only apply to the youngsters in our midst. Currently, my three daughters are working their way through adolescence, and I can tell you that they love dressing up just as much as they did when they were little. In fact, the other day my girls and I passed a formal dress shop in the mall, and without even thinking about it, we stopped at the window to *ooh* and *aah* over the gorgeous fabrics and alluring styles. Truly, women of all ages have made a pastime out of the art of dressing up.

Which raises the question: Why are we females so captivated by beautiful things, anyway? And I'm talking about more than just clothing and makeup here. We women love beauty in all its forms. We plant gardens full of flowers and decorate the walls of our homes. We quilt with attractive fabrics and create a fancy presentation for a new recipe. We even doll up our blogs with cute wallpaper and darling photos. It seems we're drawn to beauty in almost everything we do.

I believe the reason for this goes back to what we discussed in the last chapter. Remember, we are all children of heavenly parents who not only had beautiful, resurrected bodies but who were also masters at *creating* beauty. The exquisite splendor around us testifies to that. Just take in the glory of a radiant sunset, the intricacy of a delicate rosebud, or the majesty of a snow-covered mountain, and you'll see why the Psalmist says, "Out of Zion, *the perfection of beauty,* God hath shined" (Psalm 50:2; italics added). Our heavenly parents were lovers and creators of all things beautiful.

So that means creating beauty isn't simply an enjoyable pastime—it's an actual characteristic of God. Nephi taught that the tree of life was "far beyond, yea, exceeding of all beauty" (1 Nephi 11:8). I believe our Father in Heaven values beauty for a number of reasons. Of course, lovely creations are attractive and pleasing to the eye, but beauty also comforts, which is why we send flowers to the sick or those who've lost a loved one. Beauty inspires, which explains why we hang art on the walls of our home and paint murals on the walls of our temples. Also, think about how you feel when you're confronted with the breathtaking beauty in nature. Doesn't it invite you to linger, to leave behind your everyday routine, and to listen for the whisperings of the Spirit?[1] If our Father in Heaven cherishes beauty for all these reasons, then that means, as His offspring, a love of beauty is part of *our* nature as well. I'd say we're drawn to all those ballerina tutus and prom dresses because our spirits are drawn to beauty just like our heavenly parents are. It's a yearning that seems to originate in the very depths of our souls.

The problem is, we now live in a fallen world where we're saddled with a sinful natural man. As a result, we're often tempted to use our beauty for reasons that are anything but god-like. For instance, when we dress ourselves up, we may be doing so for one specific reason: to win the approval and acceptance of others. Author Michelle Graham describes a lie of the adversary that may explain why we do this:

> We all know that in our society beauty is power. The "beautiful ones" get noticed, get favored and get better treatment. . . . Being considered beautiful can mean not only better treatment but also emotional gain. There is a twisted sense of power we feel when we can make someone notice us. . . . The days that I "look good," hair done and sporting trendy clothing, I have more confidence. In my hunger for love and acceptance, *it is tempting to use my body as currency to win people over.*[2]

Have you ever used your body "as currency to win people over"? I sure have. For instance, as a young seventh-grader attending school in the southern United States, all I wanted was to own an Izod shirt. For those who didn't have the privilege of living in the '80s, Izods looked like any other collared shirt, only they had a small alligator emblem sewn on the left breast. That's it. Nothing special—just a little alligator less than an inch wide. But that alligator meant an awful lot to me. That alligator meant acceptance. It meant I would fit in. It meant I would be somebody in our little Tallahassee, Florida, junior high.

Of course, my dad couldn't fathom why I'd want to spend so much on an Izod when I could get two shirts at Kmart for the same price. "Dad," I'd groan, "Kmart shirts have foxes on them, not alligators!" The argument seems ridiculous to me now. But the point is that I was adorning my body in a way that would earn my peers' approval. I was using my body as currency to buy my way into the popular crowd.

Michelle Graham shares some penetrating insights on the inner motivation that fuels this type of behavior:

> When I use my appearance to gain the approval of others, I have taken desperate measures to fill a hole. I have become convinced that there is no other alternative. I believe that there is no other way to feel secure, affirmed and valuable. Like a hungry lion on the prowl, I am starving for love because I have fasted from divine affection.[3]

Could it be the adversary has convinced us that the only way to feel "secure, affirmed, and valuable" is to gain the acceptance of our peers? Could it be that we dress for the eyes of others in order to "fill a hole"? Maybe it's time for us to learn where our true value comes from. Maybe it's time to turn our backs on the seductive voices coming from the great and spacious building.

With that said, I want to point out that we women are often tempted to adorn ourselves not just to obtain others' approval but specifically to get the attention of *men*. After all, there's nothing quite like the feeling of capturing an attractive guy's eye. As his gaze follows us across the room, our breath catches in our throat and our heart almost skips a beat. We feel a giddy rush of excitement going from our head all the way down to our toes. It's quite an exhilarating experience. In fact, it's such a powerful feeling that even after we're married and "off the market," many of us try to recapture that moment through reading romance novels and watching chick flick DVDs. When it comes down to it, the attraction between a man and a woman is simply electric.

While there's nothing wrong with the natural magnetism that exists between the sexes, we enter the danger zone when we begin to grow attached to that feeling, when we hunger for it and feed on it from day to day. We may especially be tempted to do so once we've been married for a while and the intensity of our spouse's desire seems to have waned. It's then that we may look to other men. It may not be that we intend to be unfaithful, but simply to see if we can still turn a few heads. While that may seem like an innocent game, it's not. It's an attempt to use our physical beauty for sinful and selfish reasons.

In the Old Testament, Isaiah sent a bold warning to women of his generation who used their looks to try to draw the attention of others. Interestingly, Nephi felt impressed to add the same message to the pages of the Book of Mormon, which means that Isaiah's warning was meant for *our day* as well. It goes like this:

> Moreover, the Lord saith: Because the daughters of Zion are haughty, and walk with stretched-forth necks and wanton eyes, walking and mincing as they go, and making a tinkling with their feet—
>
> Therefore the Lord will smite with a scab the crown of the head of the daughters of Zion, and the Lord will discover their secret parts.
>
> In that day the Lord will take away the bravery of their tinkling ornaments, and cauls, and round tires like the moon;
>
> The chains and the bracelets, and the mufflers;
>
> The bonnets, and the ornaments of the legs, and the headbands, and the tablets, and the ear-rings;
>
> The rings, and nose jewels;
>
> The changeable suits of apparel, and the mantles, and the wimples, and the crisping-pins;
>
> The glasses, and the fine linen, and hoods, and the veils.
>
> And it shall come to pass, instead of sweet smell there shall be stink; and instead of a girdle, a rent; and instead of well set hair, baldness; and instead of a stomacher, a girding of sackcloth; burning instead of beauty (2 Nephi 13:16–24; see also Isaiah 3:16–24).

In the past when I read through these verses, I pictured the runway models in all their finery, and I nodded my head in agreement with the Lord's judgment on the shallow, materialistic women of the world. But one day, I saw that first verse with new eyes, and it struck me that Jehovah wasn't describing worldly women in this passage—He was speaking specifically to the "daughters of Zion," to *women of the covenant*. In that moment, this particular passage took on an entirely new meaning.

If you're wondering how Isaiah's strange words could apply to LDS women, let's review a few definitions that will make his counsel a little more relatable. First, he describes these daughters as haughty, which paints a picture of women who are conceited or arrogant, women focused solely on themselves. They use jewelry, clothing, and "well set hair" to obtain others' esteem and admiration. In addition, Isaiah mentions the "bravery" of their ornaments, but you need to know that the Hebrew word for *bravery* in this verse is *tip'eret*, which means "glory" or "splendor."[4] That means these women are dressing to be noticed. They're "walking and mincing" and stretching out their necks to see who's looking at them with respect, admiration, or even a little bit of envy.

Isaiah next speaks of "wanton eyes." The dictionary says one who's *wanton* is one who "caus[es] sexual excitement."[5] It's a woman who dresses to accentuate her curves and emphasize her features, who uses her looks to excite the hearts of men. And again, let's remember that the Lord wasn't talking about actresses or supermodels here—He was talking about *us* whenever we manipulate our appearance in order to gain the admiration, approval, or envy of anyone who will sit up and pay attention.

So, what's the Lord's warning to those of us who adorn our body with the intent of being sexually attractive to men, or to indulge our personal pride? Read again His bold declaration: "Instead of sweet smell there shall be stink; . . . instead of well set hair, baldness; and instead of a stomacher [or fine clothing[6]], a girding of sackcloth; *burning instead of beauty*" (italics added). In short, we learn here that God is very serious about the way His daughters use their physical body.

Perhaps it's time for us to ask ourselves what compels us to dress in a way that's attractive to men, or that gains the approval of our peers? What's the hole that we're so desperately trying to fill? To find out, I think it will help if we return to that pivotal moment in the Garden of Eden when Adam and Eve chose to eat the forbidden fruit. As a result of their transgression, the Father drove the two out of Eden, casting them away from their life of peace and tranquility, and cutting them off from the sustaining nourishment of the tree of life (Genesis 3:23–24).

I'll confess there's a question that's haunted me as I've pondered this particular scenario—a scenario, I might add, that also applies to you and me. The question is this: What happens to a soul that's been cut off from the tree of life? Really, what? What happens to a child who's been cut off from loving heavenly parents and their much-needed encouragement and support? To make it more personal, let me ask it this way: What happens to our heart in this "lost and fallen state" (Mosiah 16:4), a state where we've been cast out and cut off from all memory of our heavenly home?

I'd like to suggest that, because we've been cast out of our Father's presence, our heart is left with a haunting sense of emptiness, a feeling of being lost and far away from home. Though we may not even be aware of it, somewhere in our subconscious lies an inner longing that we're not quite sure how to fill. Our soul yearns to regain our Father's presence so we can find the acceptance and love we lost when we were cast out. In short, each of us hides a desperate need to find our way back home.

The trouble is, Satan knows all about this inner longing, and he uses the voices of the world to seduce us with the message: "You'll find the acceptance and approval your soul is looking for, not from God, but through the praise of the world. Join us in the great and spacious building. This is where you'll find affirmation. This is where you'll regain the acceptance you lost through the Fall. Only here will you avoid further despair and rejection. Only here will you finally feel at home."

Could it be that we're trying so hard to fit in because a home in the great and spacious building feels better than no home at all? Though we know our ultimate goal is life in the celestial kingdom, this world is our "here and now." And in the here and now, it can be painful to live with ridicule and rejection. So it can be very tempting to try to fit ourselves to the world's standard while still trying to cling to the iron rod.

If we choose to take that road, though, we've got to realize that there's a huge problem with molding ourselves to fit the worldly image of beauty. It's that "[the] image is falsehood," meaning it's a big, fat *lie* (Jeremiah 51:17). Even though we may believe that being admired and accepted will solve all our problems, we can see that lie simply isn't true. Just skim through the check-stand magazines and you'll see that the lives of the world's most popular women aren't perfect by any stretch of the imagination. Life in the great and spacious building isn't as grand as it appears to be. That's why Isaiah says "a graven image . . . is *profitable for nothing*" (Isaiah

44:10; italics added). After all, the world can't calm your anxiety, heal your sorrow, or fill you with redeeming love. The world can't carry you through tribulation, build your faith, or bring you back into the presence of God. It just goes to show that Isaiah was right. Molding ourselves to the worldly image is profitable for nothing—at least, nothing that really matters, anyway.

To add to that, when we use our bodies to gain the approval of others, we get stuck in another difficult predicament. The scriptures reveal that the "image" we've come to adore eventually becomes "a snare unto [us]" (Psalm 106:36). Now, a snare is a trap, right? It's a device that's carefully concealed by a hunter in order to quickly and easily capture his prey. If the world's standard of beauty is a snare, imagine what Satan can do with us once he gets us hooked on having the acceptance of others. Author Regina Franklin paints this all-too-familiar picture:

> Different women, different rituals. The same desire. Acceptance. Acceptance from others and from self. The woman who spins endlessly in the cycle of fad dieting in search of the perfect figure. The woman who needs expensive jewelry to feel priceless. The woman who weighs herself before and after going to the bathroom in hopes that the numbers will change. The woman who believes she is only as good as she looks. The woman who obsesses over everything she eats, calculating the calories and fat with each bite. The woman who changes her hair color to match her mood as she searches for the look that makes her feel comfortable with herself. The woman who takes diet pills to lose "just a few more pounds." The woman who cannot go out in public without makeup because she feels too vulnerable. The woman who cannot eat at public gatherings out of fear that others will judge what she eats. The woman who cannot miss a workout at the gym and who berates herself if she shortens her time on the treadmill. The woman who binges and purges, desperately seeking to control not only her weight but also her life. Different women, different rituals. The same bondage.
>
> Unhappy. Powerless. Enslaved. . . . The truth of our idolatry is poignant: we care more about what others think of us than what God thinks of us.[7]

I find it intriguing that Ms. Franklin describes these particular women as "enslaved." The reason I think it's intriguing is because her words echo something the Lord said when He revealed the Ten Commandments to Moses. Consider the very first commandment:

> I am the Lord thy God, which have brought thee out of the land of Egypt, out of the house of bondage.
>
> Thou shalt have no other gods before me.
>
> Thou shalt not make unto thee any graven image, or any likeness of any thing that is in heaven above, or that is in the earth beneath, or that is in the water under the earth:
>
> Thou shalt not bow down thyself to them, nor serve them: for I the Lord thy God am a jealous God, visiting the iniquity of the fathers upon the children unto the third and fourth generation of them that hate me. (Exodus 20:2–5)

Notice that Jehovah warned the people not to "serve" false gods or graven images. If we look at the original Hebrew word for *serve* here, we'll find that the term can actually refer to being "reduce[d] to servitude" or "enslave[d]."[8] The point that both the Lord and Regina Franklin are making is that when we worship the image in order to find acceptance, it ultimately places us in a position of *servitude*. It traps us in a snare. Even though our intentions may have begun with a simple desire to fit in or turn some heads, when we continue to imitate the ways of the world, we end up in bondage to others' opinions. And once that happens, the approval of others means more to us than the approval of God.

Now, please don't think I'm saying that we shouldn't dress or adorn our physical body in an attractive way. We already said that beauty is a natural characteristic of God, so we'll talk more later about how we can beautify our bodies in a way that is pleasing and acceptable to the Lord. But right now, we need to ask ourselves if we're using our looks to obtain the praise of the world, if we're manipulating our appearance to get the attention and affirmation of others. Regina Franklin highlights the problem with this type of behavior:

> We live in a visual culture—images elicit responses. When we strive to meet the world's standard of beauty, our bodies become images to evoke desired responses within ourselves and others. When we mold ourselves according to the world's image, *we take what God has created to be a vessel of His glory and use it instead to glorify ourselves and satisfy our desire for admiration.*[9]

It all comes down to this: if we're trying to glorify ourselves through our outward appearance, we're walking a dead-end road that will only lead to more emptiness and heartache. Truth is, there's only One who can fill our hearts with the acceptance and love we've been longing for. There's only One who can offer us the satisfying and abundant fruit of the tree of life. It's a kind of nourishment that the world can't even begin to imitate. But we can only partake of this fruit if we quit looking to other people to fill us and devote ourselves instead to seeking the acceptance and affirmation of the Lord.

For Additional Study

In Ezekiel chapter 16, the Lord compares the Israelites to a young woman. As you read verses 1–34, I want you to change the analogy in your mind so it applies to your personal involvement with the world's standard of beauty. Here are a few questions for you to consider:

- In what ways have you used your beauty to "[play] the harlot" (verse 15)? (Since a harlot exploits her beauty to make a *profit*, think about the different ways you've prof-ited or benefited from your outward appearance.)
- Have you ever used "garments" or "jewels" to draw others' attention (verses 16–17)?
- Are you tempted at times to "trust in [your] own beauty" (verse 15)?
- Would you consider your desire for others' approval to be "unsatiable" (verse 28)?
- Is it possible you sometimes take the beauty you've been given and parade it before your peers in order to obtain "renown" (verses 13–15)?

Now read verses 35–43 and ponder these final questions:

- What is the Lord's judgment on this harlot?
- Do you think there's any way such a harsh indictment could ever apply to your life? Why or why not?

Next, turn to 2 Nephi 26:29. How does the doctrine in this scripture relate to our current discussion? Now look up Galatians 1:10 and answer the same question for this verse. (Make sure to check the footnotes as you study.)

I want to close this chapter with the powerful words of Elder Jeffrey R. Holland. Evaluate how this particular quote could pertain to you personally:

> In terms of preoccupation with self and a fixation on the physical, this is more than social insanity; it is spiritually destructive, and it accounts for much of the unhappiness women, including young women, face in the modern world. And if adults are preoccupied with appearance—tucking and nipping and implanting and remodeling everything that can be remodeled—those pressures and anxieties will certainly seep through to children. At some point the problem becomes what the Book of Mormon called "vain imaginations." And in secular society both vanity and imagination run wild. One would truly need a great and spacious makeup kit to compete with beauty as portrayed in media all around us. Yet at the end of the day there would still be those "in the attitude of mocking and pointing their fingers" as Lehi saw, because however much one tries in the world of glamour and fashion, it will never be glamorous enough.[10]

Time for a Transformation

have another confession to make. For most of my life I've been a
raging chocoholic. Seriously, I'd do just about anything for some
Reese's peanut butter cups. And don't even get me started on
chocolate chip cookie dough. Or brownies layered with caramel.
Or a luscious bowl of peanut butter M&M's. The reason I feel
comfortable making this confession is because I know a lot of other
women indulge in the very same obsession. After all, I've heard
ladies joke about it in Relief Society. I've laughed with friends
about where we hide our chocolate stash. I've seen women camp
out by the chocolate fountain at parties. It's no secret that scores
of us are caught up in a love affair with this tasty little confection.

Just for fun, I searched the web and found some really amusing
results for the word *chocoholic*. My favorite was a T-shirt that read,
"Warning! I'm a woman of many moods and they all require chocolate." Another funny one was the shirt with an arrow pointing
upward that said, "In Case of Meltdown, Insert Chocolate." I also
read one news report that claimed chocolate "conjures a magical
spell over most people," and that, "among women, . . . it's craved
with such intensity that researchers believe it can be an emotion-
ally charged experience."[1] All I can say is, that's definitely been
true for me.

Now, in earlier years I might have told you I love chocolate
mainly because it tastes absolutely decadent. But over time I had to

acknowledge that this little delicacy meant much more to me than that. If the truth be told, I ate chocolate to escape. To celebrate. To calm myself when stressed. Or to entertain myself when bored. Depending on the day, chocolate was my comfort, my therapist, or my party in a little brown wrapper. Slowly it moved from being an occasional guilty pleasure to something I couldn't live without.

Yet as much as I adored this particular obsession of mine, I'll admit that not everything in my chocolate-loving heart was as it should be. Underneath all my excuses and rationalizations, I knew my chocolate consumption was getting out of control. But no matter how many times I tried to cut down, my willpower only lasted so long. Sooner or later, I'd end up scavenging through the freezer for that half-full bag of chocolate chips, or making a quick trip to Walmart where a stack of candy bars seemed to jump right into my cart. Despite my efforts to set goals, hide the treats, or keep a strict food journal, my chocolate habit was one I just couldn't seem to break.

You may be thinking, "That's very interesting, Jaci, but what in the world does your chocolate obsession have to do with our discussion on body image?" Well, I'll tell you. We've talked about how we often imitate the image in an attempt to cover the shame of being mortal, and we've also discussed how it seems to offer us the acceptance and affirmation we lost through the Fall. But I haven't yet revealed the most compelling reason I continued to chase the golden image.

In high school, it was the reason I taped a picture of a fitness model to my mirror for inspiration. In my twenties, it was the reason I watched weight-loss infomercials with such avid interest. In my thirtiess, it was the reason I checked out every "How to Drop 10 Pounds in 10 days" book in our public library. The reason was this: the image of that thin, beautiful woman represented someone who was in control of her appetite. It was the very thing I wasn't, the very thing I was desperate to become.

In short, I ran after every new diet and meal plan and workout program because I wanted to get my sweet tooth under control. I dreamt of the day I could look like the image because that would mean I'd no longer have a problem with sugar. The women in the magazines and the clothing ads—the women with the thin bodies and fresh-looking faces—represented the person I someday hoped to become. In my mind, the ideal woman maintained complete control over her physical appetite. She showed the mastery and self-discipline I so obviously lacked.

Add this reason to the other two and it's easy to see why we embrace the worldly image with such whole-hearted abandon. It's almost as if the ideal woman holds the key to our heart's deepest and most poignant desires. If we could just be more like that woman, we'd be beautiful in the eyes of others; we'd bask in their admiration and praise; we'd master our physical appetite and exhibit unending amounts of self-control. Perhaps that's the reason we sacrifice so much of our lives in pursuit of the image—because it appears to offer such abundant rewards in return. The zeal with which we pursue the image is often mind-blowing.

Which brings me to my next question: How in the world are we going to walk away from a beauty standard that's come to mean so much to us? Or to put it another way, how do we stop worshipping an image that many of us have pursued our entire lives? Should we throw out all our makeup and avoid the latest fashions? Should we repress all dreams of physical beauty and stop thinking about our appearance altogether? Should we forego all our efforts to reach a size six and reach for another candy bar as consolation?

For some reason, none of those explanations sat right with me. But if those solutions weren't the answer, then what was it? I mean, if true beauty doesn't look like a model-thin body or a wrinkle-free face, if it doesn't look like the standard of the world, then what *does* it look like for a daughter of God? I know we've heard a million times that true beauty comes from inside, and we definitely value that. But in the meantime, what did the Lord want me to do with my hair? my clothes? my face? my body? I had to do *something* with my appearance, right? While I knew that learning to control my appetite and eat in a healthier way would be a good start, my motivation was still focused on being "skinny" rather than being healthy. So how in the world could I ever begin to sort it all out? To me, these seemed like honest questions that deserved honest answers—answers I desperately needed to have before I could move on.

Deep down, I knew there had to be a way to find balance. There had to be a way to honor my God-given desire for beauty without bowing down before the image of the world. Walking away from the image couldn't mean walking away from physical attractiveness altogether. Instead, the answer had to involve learning and internalizing how the Lord understood *outward*—not just inward—beauty. I knew Christ didn't view a woman's appearance through the lens of the world, but I certainly did. For the most part, what the world saw as beautiful, I saw as beautiful, and what the world shunned, I shunned. What I needed most was a body image breakthrough. A radical change of heart. I needed the Lord to completely reframe the way I looked at physical beauty.

That meant I had a lot of work to do. After all, transforming one's body image is serious business. In the words of Patricia Holland:

> It takes constant vigilance, constant evaluation of our values and our personal needs to let go of . . . self-centeredness and live by the heart. It takes years of practice, years of prayer, meditation, and daily scripture dedication to rid ourselves of vanity's constant demands. But it is the only path to true peace, true happiness, and a constant relationship with the Lord. That is why He softly bids, 'Come unto me, . . . for I am meek and lowly in heart, and ye shall find rest unto your souls' (Matthew 11:28-29).
>
> In other words, what Christ is saying to me is, "Don't attach yourself to images and possessions and the 'plaited hair' of the world, lest they begin to mean more to you than I do, or my Father does. Let go of your ego's need for the honors that man can bestow, and I will make myself known unto you."[2]

While part of my heart thrilled at her words, another part of me struggled with feelings of fear and trepidation. I knew a body image breakthrough would involve an examination of my deepest and most cherished values and beliefs. I knew it would involve opening my heart to Christ and allowing Him access to all my heart's dirty laundry. And quite frankly, I wasn't sure I wanted to know what was buried underneath the mess. For a time, I shrunk at the thought of such a personal look into the depths of my heart.

To be perfectly honest, I *liked* the idea of being thin. I *liked* having other people's acceptance. And I *really liked* my penchant for chocolate. I wasn't sure I wanted to be transformed if it meant giving up my favorite obsessions. I mean, was I really ready to take a good, hard look at my issues with sugar or my attachment to the bathroom scale? Could I really handle seeing what was fueling my self-condemnation or driving me to make my body a smaller size? Though I knew self-examination was the first step in getting to the root of my body image problem, it was tempting to stick with dieting and dreams of thinness rather than take the time to clean out the clutter that had built up in my troubled heart.

What finally lit a spark of motivation in me was the thought that maybe, just maybe, there was a land of freedom waiting on the other side of all that dirty laundry. The prospect of shedding my obsessive thoughts, my feelings of inadequacy, and my bondage to the scale proved very enticing. Could Christ really help me discover such a place? His words assured me that it was possible.

It was as if I could hear Him say, *Jaci, don't forget, I am your Redeemer* (Mosiah 26:26). *I can cause your weary soul to rest* (Isaiah 28:12). *I can make your heart rejoice* (D&C 132:56). *I can guard your mind with peace* (Phillipians 4:7). *I can arm you with righteousness and power* (1 Nephi 14:14). *I can transform you by renewing your mind* (Romans 12:2). *I can make you forget your shame* (3 Nephi 22:4). *I can put a new spirit in you* (Ezekiel 11:19). *I can become the health of your countenance* (Psalm 42:11). *I can make your imagination mount up as on eagles' wings* (D&C 124:99). *I can break the chains that bind you* (Alma 5:9). *I can teach you the truth that sets you free* (John 8:32). *I am Jesus Christ. I came that you might have life, and have it more abundantly* (John 10:10).

I think we sometimes make the mistake of assuming these promises only apply to our inner, spiritual life, but I believe Christ can also dramatically change the way we see our *outward* appearance. I believe that because I've now experienced a body image breakthrough for myself. As a result, I can happily tell you that once you're "rooted and grounded in [Christ's] love" (Ephesians 3:17), all your self-doubt and insecurity will finally melt away for good. Rather than struggling day in and day out with feelings of shame about your physical body, the Lord can pull you out of that "horrible pit, out of the miry clay, and set [your] feet on a rock" (Psalm 40:2). Remember, this is *His* rock we're talking about, "a foundation whereon if [you] build [you] cannot fall" (Helaman 5:12).

Please believe me when I say that if you'll simply allow the Lord to lead you through the transformation process, you'll discover a new place to live—a place where you'll actually *rejoice* in your physical body. It's a place where you'll find the ability to master your appetite; where your weight will settle in at a healthy level; and where all obsessive thinking will finally cease. Best of all, it's a place where you'll come to know the beauty and splendor of Christ, and how it applies to *your* individual body. I promise, it's a place unlike anything you've ever experienced.

However, the only way you can enter this brave new world is by working your way through a number of important steps. Yes, you'll have to shed some baggage along the way, but I assure you the rewards will be worth it. It'll be worth it because you'll eventually become a different person, one who is no longer controlled by food, the pressure to be thin, or a need to resemble the image. What I'm describing here is a woman who truly knows who she is—an incredibly beautiful daughter of God. It's a life that's out there waiting for each of us—if we'll exercise the faith to reach out and take the Master's hand.

So tell me: Are you ready to quit bowing before the worldly image? Are you ready to walk a new path and carve out a new destiny, not only for yourself but also for the daughters and granddaughters who will be blessed by your influence? Are you ready to join me as we learn how to define ourselves by the Lord's standard of beauty rather than that of the world?

It's time, you know. Time to understand who you really are. Time to get out from underneath the enemy's thumb. Time to "awake" and "put on thy beautiful garments," to "shake thyself from the dust" and "loose thyself from the bands of thy neck, O captive daughter of Zion" (2 Nephi 8:24–25). Like Shadrach, Meshach, and Abed-nego, it's time to turn our backs on the golden image of the world.

For Additional Study

The scriptures at times speak of those who are unwilling to admit, or turn from, their idolatrous worship. For example, read Jeremiah chapter 2 and answer the following questions:

- In what ways does the worldly standard of beauty resemble a "broken cistern" (verse 13)?
- Is it possible you have "changed [your] gods" for an image that "doth not profit" (verse 11)?
- What does Jeremiah say in verse 23 about living in denial of our idolatry?
- How would you relate the question in verse 36 to your feelings about your physical body?

Next, let's look at the transformation that Alma speaks of in the Book of Mormon. Read through Alma 5:7–14 and think about how we can apply these verses to our struggle with body image:

- In what ways do your negative thoughts and feelings about your body resemble "the bands of death, and the chains of hell" (verse 7)?
- What was it that set the people free from these miserable chains (see verse 12)?
- How exactly does Alma describe their deliverance in verses 7 and 14?
- How do you think these verses could apply to your battle with your body image?

Finally, turn to Psalm 40:1–3. Consider the imagery David uses and tell me:

- In what ways have your feelings about your body trapped you in a "horrible pit"?
- What happened when David cried out to the Lord for mercy?
- How would it feel to have your feet "set . . . upon a rock" when it comes to your body image?
- What do you think it means to have a "new song [put] in [your] mouth"?

It's All in Our Heads

The title of this chapter is taken from one of my husband's favorite ways to tease me. Whenever I'm rambling on about some concern in my life, he gets this sly little grin on his face and he says, "Hon, it's all in your head." Of course, I can't help but repeat it back to him when it's his turn to vent. Though it's only a joke for Greg and me, there's actually a lot of truth in that little statement. If we're ever going to stop bowing before the image, the first thing we need to do is take a good look at what's going on in our head.

In her insightful book, *Through His Eyes: Rethinking What You Believe About Yourself*, author Virginia H. Pearce talks about our Belief Box, a term she uses to represent the part of our mind that houses our thoughts and beliefs. Sister Pearce points out that, in this Box, there are three compartments or types of beliefs: Truths with a capital *T* (eternal truths), truths with a lowercase *t* (bits of wisdom or good advice), and beliefs that are not true at all. This last category, she says, "is quite important, because not all of our beliefs are true. Some are actually lies."[1] With regard to these lies, Sister Pearce explains,

> We are generally unaware that such ideas are in our Belief Box, because when we dig everything out and look at them, they don't make sense. In fact, they are laughable. Unfortunately, however, they can be very powerful in determining our emotions and our behavior.[2]

In her words we learn one possible reason for our negative body image: we have a whole bunch of debilitating lies running around in our head. The trouble is, we've never allowed ourselves to admit that these lies exist. So the first step in the transformation process is to evaluate every single thing we believe about our physical body. We need to uncover any beliefs that, under scrutiny, would prove to be lies rather than truth.

Here's how Sister Pearce suggests we begin:

> Listen to the chatter in your head. Don't talk back or make any judgments. Just listen. Slip into your "observing self" as you become aware of strong emotions—positive or negative—and try to hear the chatter that created those emotions. Don't do anything about it yet. Just watch and let it be. It's pretty interesting. Much more entertaining than watching reality television![3]

Did you notice how she said our strong emotions are "created" by the chatter in our head? It just goes to show what a powerful connection there is between our thoughts, beliefs, and emotions. After all, once we *believe* an idea is true, our feelings jump on board to support that same idea, even if it it's not true at all. Let me show you a few simple examples and I think you'll see what Sister Pearce is talking about.

Let's say we tune in to the "chatter" in our head, and we find it sounds something like this:

- I believe I'll never be able to conquer my issues with food.
- I believe I must be thin to have worth as a woman.
- I believe my husband is addicted to pornography because I'm not good enough.
- I believe that if I don't continue to diet, I'll never stop gaining weight.
- I believe most of my problems are related to the way I look.

We'll talk later about where these kinds of ideas come from, but for now, I want to repeat those five statements again, and after each one, I'm going to add some emotions that can be created by these kinds of false beliefs:

- I believe I'll never be able to conquer my issues with food, which leaves me feeling hopeless, weak, discouraged, desperate, and miserable.

- I believe I must be thin to have worth as a woman, which leaves me feeling worthless, insignificant, invisible, useless, and inadequate.
- I believe my husband is addicted to pornography because I'm not good enough, which leaves me feeling ugly, repulsive, ashamed, rejected, and unwanted.
- I believe that if I don't continue to diet, I'll never stop gaining weight, which leaves me feeling guilty, trapped, frustrated, irritated, and exhausted.
- I believe most of my problems are related to how I look, which leaves me feeling angry, resentful, bitter, powerless, and downhearted.

Let's be honest, none of us like to experience these kinds of crippling emotions. You'd think we'd drop our false beliefs because they cause us so much pain. However, most of the time, we don't. Have you ever wondered why that is? Perhaps one reason we cling to the lies in our head is because our persuasive emotions make them *feel* true, even though they aren't. Sister Pearce adds this important insight:

> Some of the not-true-at-all beliefs we hold are so powerful that we simply don't 'see' or allow in any data that doesn't support them. We ignore conflicting experiences and give extra weight to those experiences that confirm the erroneous beliefs we have come to cherish—even while they cause pain and unhappiness.[4]

I want to repeat that one more time to make sure we don't miss it. We often choose to cherish our false beliefs *even though they cause us pain and unhappiness*. I know it's an irrational way to live, but I'm guessing most of us have watched ourselves repeat this pattern over and over again, trapping us in beliefs and emotions that we'd very much like to escape.

To illustrate, let me show you one way this pattern played out in my personal life. The story starts quite simply: the summer after my senior year, I made a rash decision to chop off all my hair. At the time, I really loved my new short cut because it was really easy to style. A few weeks later, I left for Ricks College (now BYU-Idaho), and it wasn't long before I met Greg, the man who would become my husband.

One day, as Greg and I were looking through some high school photos, we came across a few of my senior pictures. To my surprise, he went nuts talking about how much he loved my long hair. Though he never said anything negative about my short cut, it was immediately obvious which one he preferred. Needless to say, that very day I committed to growing my hair out as quickly as possible. As a soon-to-be bride, I wanted very much to please Greg, to be seen as beautiful in my husband's eyes.

What I never realized at the time was that one simple experience created within me the belief that I was only attractive with long hair—the shorter my hair got, the uglier I got. The crazy thing is, my sweet husband never implied anything of the sort. (After all, he *married* me with short hair, so it couldn't have been that bad!) No, this particular false belief came solely as a result of the way I twisted that conversation in my own mind. Though I never put this powerful belief into words, it served as the foundation for how I handled my hair for years to come.

For example, a few years later when my hair had finally reached my shoulders, I went to our local beauty college for a trim. The stylist misunderstood what I asked for and cut off about two inches. I did what any self-respecting woman does after a horrible salon experience—I went home and cried my eyes out. My husband was baffled and said, "Jaci, it's only hair. It'll grow back." What he didn't know was that, to me, it was much more than hair. Because of the belief I held that my worth was tied to the length of my hair, it felt like the stylist stole my beauty and left me as an ugly duckling. In my mind, it was impossible for me to be attractive with such short hair. It just goes to show how dramatically one false belief can influence our thoughts, our feelings, our actions—even our very lives.

I found another example of the power of false beliefs in the book *Love to Eat, Hate to Eat: Breaking the Bondage of Destructive Eating Habits.* In one chapter, Christian author Elyse Fitzpatrick described a bulimic woman who lived her life by one very compelling false belief—she had to be thinner than her sisters:

She had first embraced this thought in junior high and had never really grown past it. "*I must be thinner than my sisters,*" was so strong in her desires that it actually functioned as a god to her, even though she wasn't always fully aware of it. Her obsession dictated the focus of her thoughts and actions. . . .

Her daily experience of peace and joy was determined by whether she was "good"or "bad" in her eating. Her emotions alternated between anger and frustration because she spent her life in such futility; she felt depressed and fearful that she would never change, and she was filled with self-loathing and self-indulgence. These emotions gave rise to more despair, disgust, and bitterness, leading her to eat everything in sight. [She] wanted to serve the Lord and after each binge, she would resolve again to live her life for Christ. But she continually found her thoughts focused on the questions, *What do I look like? Am I gaining weight? Am I as good as they are?* As a result, her relationships with her family were affected. Every family gathering was ruined by fear. When [she] saw her sisters she immediately compared herself with them—had they gained weight? Was she more in control than they? Did they compliment her on her figure? Would they criticize her for being too thin or too fat? . . . Would they eat two helpings of turkey? She would have only one . . . did they notice?[5]

Any chance you recognize yourself in some part of this story? Though the specifics may be a little different, the important thing we need to realize is that all of this woman's torment—all of her fear, depression, self-loathing, and despair—came because of one false belief. Don't forget, even though her experience was *real*, it still wasn't based on *truth*. Instead, her thoughts, feelings, and emotions were all founded on a big, fat lie. The repercussions of what goes on in our head are enormous. We'll never be transformed until these kinds of erroneous beliefs are eradicated from our hearts and minds. Whether we struggle with something simple like my issue with hair or something more complicated like this woman's story, the battle for freedom ultimately begins inside our own heads. Sooner or later, all our false beliefs must be cast out, disassembled, sent to the trash where they belong.

The problem is, if you're anything like me, you've discovered that's much easier said than done. Even if we understand intellectually that a belief isn't true, it's another thing entirely to stop believing it, stop feeling the emotions attached to it, and stop acting out the behaviors that reinforce it. Personally, I've watched myself try over and over again to change the way I think and feel, without any lasting success. Often, I've just felt stuck, chained to my irrational but very persuasive false beliefs.

This inner struggle reminds me of a clip I watched on YouTube several years ago. In this *Mad TV* skit, actor Bob Newhart plays a therapist who's counseling a new patient. As he invites the woman to sit down, Newhart tells her that he only charges for the first five minutes, hinting that he can cure any problem she has in that amount of time. The woman begins telling him that she suffers from a strange fear of being buried alive in a box. She confesses that this fear is making her life horrible, that it's keeping her from doing things she would otherwise enjoy, and that she'd like very much to overcome it. Bob listens carefully and then tells the woman, "I'm going to say two words to you right now. I want you to listen to them very, very carefully. Then I want you to take them out of the office with you, and incorporate them into your life." As she eagerly awaits his life-changing counsel, Newhart leans forward and says, "You ready? Okay, here they are: *STOP IT!*"[6]

The reason this clip has received over a million hits on YouTube isn't just because it's funny, but because we've all been there. We've heard the crazy chatter in our head, we've felt the depression and hopelessness, and we've watched ourselves act in irrational ways. And we'd love to take Bob up on his advice and just *stop it*. But for some reason, we can't. No matter how hard we try, we can't let go of certain thoughts and feelings. They feel too big, too consuming, and too important to just throw away. So the question is: How do we cast out the false beliefs in our head for good? How do we get past the point of simply recognizing the lies, and begin to take them apart instead? In the end, this is something we've got to know if we're ever going to see our physical appearance in a whole new light.

For me, a realization came as I pondered something Jesus did again and again throughout His earthly ministry. He cast out devils. Over and over He rid tortured souls of the evil influence that held them captive (for instance, see Matthew 8:16 and Mark 1:34). He even cast seven devils out of Mary Magdalene, the woman who'd be the first to witness His resurrection (Mark 16:9, John 20:11–17). It's something that seemed to pop up almost everywhere He went.

Yet strangely, we never hear any sacrament meeting talks or Relief Society lessons today on casting out devils. In fact, I don't think I've ever heard a testimony of one who's experienced such a liberation. This disconnect between Christ's day and ours has made me wonder: Were the Jewish people more prone to "unclean spirits" than we are (Luke 6:18)? Or could it be that in our day the adversary's minions have simply gone underground? Perhaps because we no longer talk about having any devils to cast out, we're less prone to recognize a false spirit's powerful influence for what it is.

In fact, I'd like to suggest it's time for us to consider where the negative voices and false beliefs in our head are coming from. Could it be that Satan and his minions have more to do with our negative body image than we think? Could it be, like Mary Magdalene, we also need help casting out a few devils? After all, we haven't had much luck doing it on our own. Maybe there's more we could learn from the One who knew exactly how to free our minds from all unwanted influences and debilitating false beliefs.

It turns out that Jesus's disciples needed His help to accomplish this very task. When Christ came back into town after the Mount of Transfiguration, a desperate father broke through the crowd, fell at His feet, and pled with Him, "Lord, have mercy on my son: for he is a lunatic, and sore vexed. . . . And I brought him to thy disciples, and they could not cure him" (Matthew 17:15–16). Quickly, Jesus asked for the boy, rebuked the devil, and "the child was cured from that very hour" (Matthew 17:18).

However, the part of the story that interests us comes later when, in a private moment, the frustrated disciples asked, "Why could not we cast him out?" (verse 19). After chiding the men for their lack of faith, Christ provided one simple caveat that will give us the insight we need most at this point in the transformation process: "Howbeit this kind goeth not out but by *prayer* and *fasting*" (verse 21; italics added).

If, like me, you've had trouble casting out your body image demons, if, like me, you've failed again and again in the heat of such a battle, Jesus gives us the answer to success in this one short verse. Only through prayer and fasting will we finally break free from the power of the image. Only through prayer and fasting will we cast out our false beliefs and crippling emotions. Only through prayer and fasting will we be set free from the awful chains that bind us.

But just in case these two spiritual disciplines have become a little too familiar to you—just in case you're contemplating a simple "Heavenly Father, please help me" and a few fast Sundays without meals—let me tell you right now that we're about to go a whole lot deeper than that. In fact, it's my hope that, after we spend the next few chapters discussing a new way to look at both prayer and fasting, you'll feel your body image breakthrough finally taking place in your own mind and heart.

For Additional Study

Take a minute to read through Ephesians 4:17–25. After you've done so, ponder the following questions:

- What do you think it means to "walk in the vanity of [your] mind" (verse 17)? (Note that the word *vain* means "excessively proud of *or concerned about* one's own appearance.")[7]
- In what ways do you think the worldly image of beauty "[alienates you] from the life of God"? (verse 18)
- What have you "heard" and "been taught by [the Lord]" about your physical body? (verse 21)
- Could it be that the "conversation [of] the old man" that you need to "put off" is the harmful or distracting conversation going on in your head? (verse 22)

Paul also tells us in this chapter that we need to be "renewed in the spirit of [our] mind" (verse 23). Some of the synonyms for the word *renew* include regenerate, replace, rebuild, restore, refresh, renovate, rejuvenate, replenish, and revive.[8] Now answer these questions:

- How do you think these hopeful, encouraging words could apply to the thought patterns of your mind regarding your physical body?
- In order to be renewed, how can you begin to "[put] away [the] lying" that's happening inside your mind? (verse 25)
- How do you "put on the new man" when it comes to your feelings about your physical body? (verse 24) (We'll talk more about all of these questions in an upcoming chapter.)

To learn more about how Satan and other false spirits may have influenced your negative body image, read the following scriptures: 1 Timothy 4:1; 1 Nephi 11:31; Mosiah 3:6; Moroni 7:17; Doctrine and Covenants 46:7; Doctrine and Covenants 50:1–3; and Doctrine and Covenants 93:24–25. Notice how the verses in 1 Timothy and Doctrine and Covenants 46 both speak of "seducing spirits." Also, note in 1 Timothy 4:1, the footnote on the word *seducing* says "deceitful." The dictionary says the word *deceive* means "to cause to accept as true or valid what is false or invalid; [to impose] a false idea or belief that causes ignorance, bewilderment, or helplessness."[9] With that said, consider these final questions:

In what ways has the devil and his angels convinced you to "accept as true" things that are "false or invalid"? For instance, have they whispered lies into your mind through the words of others, or through the media? Or have they influenced you through the thoughts and feelings of your heart?

Do you ever feel helpless to overcome your negative body image? Would you like to break free from these seemingly indestructible chains? (If so, keep reading. That's exactly where we're headed.)

A Lesson from the Book of Psalms

et's start with the concept of prayer. I'm guessing that, if you grew up in an LDS home, you learned to pray at a very young age. Greg and I taught our children to fold their arms for prayer even before they could talk. It's such a foundational element of the gospel of Jesus Christ that, by adulthood, most of us have probably offered thousands of prayers. We know the pattern well: Address our Father. Thank Him for blessings. Ask for our needs. Then close in the name of Jesus Christ. So what more really needs to be said in a chapter on prayer? A lot, actually.

In fact, I believe the only way we can transform the way we see our body is by incorporating three very specific things into our prayers. We'll find these key elements beautifully illustrated in the pages of the Old Testament. Come with me as we listen to David pour out his heart to God through Psalms. As we follow the great shepherd-king's example, we'll take our first steps in ridding ourselves of the false beliefs that are fueling our negative body image.

Find False Beliefs

First, read David's lament in Psalms 19 and 26:

Who can understand his errors? cleanse thou me from secret faults. Keep back thy servant from presumptuous sins; let them not have dominion over me (Psalm 19:12–13). Examine me, O Lord, and prove me; try my reins and my heart (Psalm 26:2).

It might help to know that the Hebrew word for "reins" in the second line is *kilya*, which refers to "the seat of thought and emotion of the inner person."[1] That means David is pleading for the Lord to help him understand the secret faults of his mind and heart, to dig below the surface and uncover all the errors hiding underneath his conscious thought. This type of prayer is crucial because our Savior knows us much better than we know ourselves. He sees things hiding in our heart that we can't see. So the best way to clean out our body image clutter is to ask Him to show us where to start.

The prophet Jeremiah echoed this same type of prayer when he said, "O Lord, I know that the way of man is not in himself: it is not in man that walketh to direct his steps." Then he continued, "O Lord, correct me, but with judgment; not in thine anger, lest thou bring me to nothing" (Jeremiah 10:23–24). Here Jeremiah acknowledged that he didn't have it in him to guide or direct his own path, and that he needed help in order to think and act in a way that was pleasing to God.

Once I began to ask the Lord to examine my mind and heart, I noticed that His process in answering this prayer was two-fold. First, working through the power of the Spirit, He turned a spotlight on every single lie that lived inside my heart and head. Second, He made sure I understood how each of those lies came to be. Eventually, I realized the only way I could cast out my false beliefs was to learn how I accumulated those misleading beliefs in the first place. Tracing each lie back to its original roots allowed me to weed out the falsehoods and prepare the soil of my mind for new seeds of truth. This is a process you must also go through if you want to experience a body image breakthrough for yourself.

False beliefs can actually be planted in the soil of our mind in a number of different ways. Dr. Deborah Newman, author of *Loving Your Body*, explains it like this:

> You developed your opinions about your body through various senses and experiences over the years. There are five main senses and experiences through which you gather the data that sums up your body image. Your body image consists of:
>
> > visual information (what you see);

mental information (what you think about what you see);

emotional information (feelings you associate with how you look);

kinetic information (how your body functions and moves); and

historical information (what you remember about how others have reacted to your body). . . .

It's critical for you to acknowledge how often your negative body image has been reinforced over your lifetime. When a statement is reinforced over and over, it takes on a sense of truth, even if it is not true. Negative feelings, experiences, and comments combine into a powerful force that blinds you from seeing who you really are.[2]

That's why we need the Lord to examine our mind and heart. We've subconsciously adopted false messages through these five avenues, and we need our Savior to help us see not just the lies but also the sandy foundation on which those lies are built. For instance, I never understood why I felt so insecure about short hair until the Lord reminded me what happened that day Greg and I were looking at my senior pictures. It was a powerful *aha* moment that inspired me to look for all the false beliefs hiding deep inside my head.

Your *aha* moment may come when the Sprit traces your body image lies back to the way your brother teased you or a family member embarrassed you about your weight. Maybe your lies were born the first time you looked in the mirror after having a baby, or the day you tried on every swimsuit in the store and nothing fit. Perhaps your lies originated in your youth when a boy rejected you and broke your heart, or when your parents went through a messy divorce. Satan and his forces use negative experiences like these to sow false truths deep within the recesses of your mind. But no matter how your false beliefs originated, the key is to let the Lord take you back to the beginning of every single falsehood. Only as you come to see "things as they really are" will you finally begin the path to true and lasting healing (Jacob 4:13).

Confess False Beliefs and Secret Faults

Once the Spirit begins to reveal the secret faults and errors living inside our minds, the next element we need to add to our prayers is *confession*. Interestingly, the Greek word for *confess* is *homologeo*, which means "to acknowledge, . . . admit, [or] declare."[3] When we confess our false beliefs, what we're really doing is admitting to God that we've adopted—and acted on—lies rather than truth.

Confession is crucial because, at some point, we may be tempted to disregard the Spirit's promptings, or to wrestle and argue with what the Lord is trying to tell us. When confronted with our false beliefs, we may want to drum up excuses, justify our actions, or even continue living in denial. But rather than fighting against the Lord throughout the transformation process, our goal should be to offer a humble, submissive spirit—to willingly agree with whatever we're being taught about the thoughts, and especially sins, lurking in the corners of our hearts and minds.

There's another temptation that often arises when we uncover certain false beliefs. If we determine that some of those beliefs came as a result of the hurtful words and actions of others, we may want to blame them for our poor body image, thus relieving ourselves of any responsibility for the problem. We need to remember that, even though others may have been cruel or unkind to us in the past, *we* were the ones who chose what thoughts to foster in our mind and *we* were the ones who acted on lies rather than truth. Thus the need for confession. It's the way we take responsibility for the lies that have been living quietly inside our head. Only as we hold ourselves accountable for our own sinful thoughts can we finally move forward in the transformation process.

Notice how David displayed this type of contrite spirit:

> I acknowledged my sin unto thee, and mine iniquity have I not hid. I said, I will confess my transgressions unto the Lord; and thou forgavest the iniquity of my sin. (Psalm 32:5) I will declare mine iniquity; I will be sorry for my sin. (Psalm 38:18)

Above all, we must realize that confession isn't simply a helpful suggestion or a nice idea, it's actually a commandment from the Lord. Recall His bold words in the Doctrine and Covenants: "Wherefore, I command you again to repent, lest I humble you with my almighty power; and that you *confess your sins*, lest you suffer these punishments of which I have spoken" (D&C 19:20; italics added).

I encourage you, as you kneel down to pray, to pour out your thoughts and feelings without holding anything back. Acknowledge the many ways you've adopted the world's standard as your own. Declare how you've bowed before the image, not only in your thoughts and feelings but in your actions as well. Don't hide your sins, but confess them—both to the Lord, and to yourself.

Perhaps you'll confess that you are way too attached to the bathroom scale; that you've used food as your comfort rather than turning to God; that you've relied on your looks to get attention from men; or that you've spent your days cursing your precious body rather than showing gratitude for it. It could be you'll confess a problem with bulimia, an obsessive need to count every calorie you eat, or a neglect of the healthy practices that would keep your body strong. Whatever body image issues you struggle with, it's vital that you confess these concerns fully and completely in your personal prayers.

I have to say, one of the things that shocked me most about adding confession to my prayers was the way it made me feel. Surprisingly, the sense of honesty and vulnerability that accompanied my confession actually drew me *closer* to my Savior rather than making me shrink back in shame. What's more, by pulling my false beliefs out of their hiding place and acknowledging them freely before the Lord, it allowed me to rip those lies off the walls of my mind and create a clean slate on which the Spirit could write. The process was liberating, not awkward; healing, not embarrassing. In fact, it's a process I still actively practice to this very day.

Plead for Grace

With those two steps firmly in place, it's time to add the final element to our prayers—grace. I'm smiling as I write this because I think this one is the most beautiful of all. Again, I'll let David express it because he has such a wonderful way with words:

> Have mercy upon me, O God, according to thy loving kindness: according unto the multitude of thy tender mercies blot out my transgressions.

Wash me throughly from mine iniquity, and cleanse me from my sin. . . .

Behold, thou desirest truth in the inward parts: and in the hidden part thou shalt make me to know wisdom.

Purge me with hyssop, and I shall be clean: wash me, and I shall be whiter than snow.

Make me to hear joy and gladness; that the bones which thou hast broken may rejoice.

Hide thy face from my sins, and blot out all mine iniquities.

Create in me a clean heart, O God; and renew a right spirit within me.

Cast me not away from thy presence; and take not thy holy spirit from me.

Restore unto me the joy of thy salvation; and uphold me with thy free spirit (Psalm 51:1–2, 6–12).

Do David's words make your heart sing like they do mine? Here's where the sweet power of Christ comes in (although He's actually been helping us all along). Here's where we plead for the Lord to change us, to give us a "clean heart," a new heart, a heart like His. And the only way we can get such a heart is to be filled with our Savior's amazing grace.

I'm sure you've heard that the Lord's grace is an "enabling power" that gives us "strength and assistance to do good works that [we] otherwise would not be able to maintain if left to [our] own means."[4] Wouldn't you agree that, when it comes to our body image, we need power far beyond our own? We need it because salvation—including salvation from our negative body image—comes only "through the merits, and mercy, and grace of the Holy Messiah" (2 Nephi 2:8). Only Christ has the power to break the chains that hold us captive.

Like David, our goal at this point is to plead with all our heart for the Lord to pour out His sustaining grace, to beg Him to wash us from our iniquity and cleanse us from our sin. We've seen our failures as we've tried to cast out the lies and heal ourselves. It's time for us to acknowledge with Ammon, "Yea, I know I am nothing; as to my strength I am weak; therefore I will boast of my God, for in his strength I can do all things" (Alma 26:12).

In answer to our heartfelt prayer, the Lord will grant us His grace in a number of ways throughout the transformation process. Initially, His enabling power will enter our minds and help us smash our false beliefs into tiny little pieces. Next, we'll watch in awe as He teaches us how to reframe and rework everything we believe about our physical body. As this process continues, we'll rejoice as we feel His love dissolving our self-condemnation once and for all. In the end, it's all part of the "change of heart" we're promised in the pages of the Book of Mormon (Alma 5:26).

More than anything, we must understand that accessing the Savior's grace is the only way we can turn the corner in our body image transformation. Only as we experience Christ's transcendent power can we truly be "made free" from the lies that have run rampant in our head (Mosiah 5:8). The good news is that even though we still have more work to do, we're now clearly on our way. It won't be long until we're living the life of a magnificently beautiful daughter of God.

For Additional Study

As the Lord begins to unveil the false beliefs hiding inside your head, I think it's helpful to journal all the negative thoughts and the feelings that you've been struggling with. Take a moment to consider what your false beliefs have cost you. For example, what affect have they had on your marriage? your children? your personal sense of worth?

Turn to Doctrine and Covenants 59:8 and think about the sacrifice the Lord is asking for in this verse. How do you think confession relates to having a broken heart and contrite spirit? Read 2 Nephi 4:16–35 and Ether 3:2. What do Nephi and the brother of Jared teach us about confession? For further study on a broken heart and contrite spirit, read Psalm 34:18; Isaiah 57:15; 2 Nephi 2:7; Doctrine and Covenants 56:18; and Doctrine and Covenants 97:8. What do these verses reveal about how we find salvation from our negative body image?

Perhaps one lie many of us need to confess is the belief that nothing can ever heal our body image—not even the Atonement of Jesus Christ. If this lie has lived in your heart, ask yourself why you've come to feel this way. What causes you to hold on to such a dangerous lie? Perhaps it would help to study scriptures on faith in the Topical Guide. Also, let me share the insightful words of Christian author Oswald Chambers. In reference to John 4:11 where the woman at the well tells Christ the well is deep, Chambers shares this profound insight:

> Think of the depths of human nature and human life; think of the depth of the "wells" in you. Have you been limiting, or impoverishing, the ministry of Jesus to the point that He is unable to work in your life? Suppose you have a deep "well" of hurt and trouble inside your heart, and Jesus comes and says to you, "Let not your heart be troubled . . ." (John 14:1). Would your response be to shrug your shoulders and say, "But, Lord, the well is too deep, and even You can't draw up quietness and comfort out of it." . . . We limit the Holy One of Israel by remembering only what we have allowed Him to do for us in the past, and also by saying, "Of course, I cannot expect God to do this particular thing." *The thing that approaches the very limits of His power is the very thing we as disciples of Jesus ought to believe He will do.* We impoverish and weaken His ministry in us the moment we forget He is almighty. The impoverishment is in us, not in Him. We will come to Jesus for Him to be our comforter or our sympathizer, *but we refrain from approaching Him as our Almighty God.*[5]

As you continue to look deep inside your heart, another important step is to recognize any resentment you may feel toward those who caused you to harbor negative feelings for your physical body. If you continue to foster these bitter feelings, all it will do is poison your heart and keep you from moving forward. Thus, your goal at this point is to forgive. I believe that's another reason we need the Lord's redeeming grace: so we can find the strength to forgive those who've hurt, rejected, or wounded us in any way.

Return to Psalm 51 and look at the first phrase of verse 1. What is David asking for in this verse? Now read the following scriptures: Luke 18:13; Mosiah 4:2; and Alma 34:17; 36:18; and 38:8. Why do you think the Lord's mercy is such a precious gift? In what ways do you think your Savior will manifest His mercy when it comes to your view of your physical body?

Burying Our Swords

Are you ready to move on to fasting? As with prayer, fasting is a concept we Mormons understand well. For most of us, it probably conjures up thoughts of hiding our rumbling stomach on fast Sunday or simply trying to go twenty-four hours without food. But if you'll let me, I'd like to take this practice beyond those ordinary limits, because in our case, fasting needs to be about much more than missing a couple of meals.

Let me begin by showing you a few verses in the Doctrine and Covenants. In section 59, we're taught that "on this, the Lord's day, thou shalt offer thine oblations and thy sacraments unto the Most High, confessing thy sins unto thy brethren, and before the Lord" (D&C 59:12). (I hope you didn't miss the "confessing" part of that verse!) Now pay attention to the counsel that comes next: "And on this day thou shalt do none other thing, only let thy food be prepared with singleness of heart that thy fasting may be perfect, or, in other words, that thy joy may be full" (verse 13). Did you notice anything odd in that scripture? The Savior said to prepare our *food* with singleness of heart, that our *fasting* may be perfect. Anyone else think that's a little weird? Why would we be preparing a meal if we're fasting? Maybe the fasting the Lord is talking about here has nothing to do with what we eat.

To prove my point, grab your scriptures and glance at footnote *a* in verse 13. What does it say? In this verse, fasting is equated with "hungering and thirsting after righteousness." Wouldn't you agree that would involve much more than just not eating? Hungering and thirsting after righteousness involves directing our yearnings and longings away from ourselves and toward the Lord. It involves "cleav[ing] unto him . . . with all [our] heart and with all [our] soul" (Joshua 22:5). And it involves "lay[ing] aside the things of this world, and seek[ing] for the things of a better" (D&C 25:10).

Another way to describe this kind of fasting is with the word *abstain*. Webster says *abstain* means, "to refrain deliberately and often with an effort of self-denial from an action or practice."[1] When we abstain, we're voluntarily denying ourselves certain things in order to devote ourselves more fully to God. And note that it's often an "action or practice" we're setting aside, not just food and drink. It reminds me of the spirit of Lent we discussed in an earlier chapter.

A great example of this type of fasting or abstaining is found in the Book of Mormon. When the people of Anti-Nephi-Lehi were converted to the gospel, they wanted to do something tangible to demonstrate their faith and commitment to the Lord. So they gathered their swords, dug a huge hole, and buried their weapons deep in the earth. Notice that the people chose to *abstain* from all their warring—to bury that which was leading them to sin (Alma 24:17–18). And that's our main goal at this point as well. It's time for us to fast from all reminders of the image. To metaphorically bury everything image-related that's causing us to sin.

One of the first things I chose to fast from was specific kinds of media. I chose this because I'm a bit of a fitness buff, which isn't a bad thing, but I realized I was spending way too much time taking in the world's views on working out and getting in shape. So I decided to lay aside the health magazines, put down the fitness books, and quit surfing the workout websites. Please understand, I didn't do this because these things are sinful in and of themselves; I did it because, through these outlets, the message of the image was dominating my thoughts and keeping me from having a mind "single to the glory of God" (D&C 88:68). Like the people of Anti-Nephi-Lehi, I knew the only way to devote myself to the Lord was to fast. Remember, this kind of fasting isn't about food—it's about separating ourselves from the things of the world. It's about doing all we can to stifle the voices in the great and spacious building. It's about choosing to cut ourselves off from all the mind-infiltrating propaganda of the image.

You might be wondering how this concept will apply to you in your own life. All I can say is, that's ultimately between you and the Lord. Perhaps you'll be prompted to fast from TV shows that promote the worldly image of beauty. Perhaps you'll "bury" your credit cards or avoid certain stores whenever you visit the mall. Perhaps you'll stop visiting certain sites on the Internet or you'll avert your eyes every time you go through the checkout stand. Perhaps, like me, you'll stop weighing yourself altogether because the scale wields too much power over your daily moods. You may even choose all of the above. But no matter how you fast, I promise that as you ask for the Spirit's guidance, He'll show you how to stop the worldly voices from worming their way into your head.

You might be surprised to learn that Jehovah commanded this kind of abstinence from the Israelites when they entered the land of Canaan. While He'd assured the people that they would inherit the Promised Land, at the time it was completely overrun with pagan images. So the Lord gave the children of Israel these important instructions:

> Take heed to thyself, lest thou make a covenant with the inhabitants of the land whither thou goest, lest it be for a snare in the midst of thee:
> But ye shall destroy their altars, break their images, and cut down their groves:
> For thou shalt worship no other god: for the Lord, whose name is Jealous, is a jealous God. (Exodus 34:12–14)

Notice that Jehovah didn't say, "Do your best not to be affected by their idols," or "Make sure to limit the time you spend around them," or "All things in moderation." Instead, His direction was clear: destroy those dangerous images—break them in pieces and cut them down. Now, I know the images in our day look very different from the ones in Canaan, but the underlying counsel remains the same. Just like the Israelites, we too must "put away the strange gods that are among [us]" (Genesis 35:2). In vivid and even humorous words that women especially understand, Isaiah tells us that we must "defile . . . [our] graven images . . . [and] cast them away as a menstruous cloth; [we must] say unto it, Get thee hence" (Isaiah 30:22).

I want to share another thing the Spirit prompted me to bury deep in the earth, but I'll admit that I'm a little hesitant to mention it. That's because every time I do, I get raised eyebrows or strange looks. Yet I feel like I need to bring it up anyway, because it's something that's made a huge difference in my daily life. The thing I needed to fast from was my obsession for chocolate.

Why would I do such a thing? Well, I've already admitted that, for me, chocolate was not just an occasional treat, but an escape, a comfort, a therapist, and even a friend. And it never crossed my mind that there was anything wrong with that. But the Spirit showed me it was a problem for a number of reasons. First, I needed to realize that chocolate was actually functioning as a redeemer or deliverer in my everyday life. In short, that tiny little treat had become a full-blown false god.

I know that sounds odd, but think for a minute about what a redeemer does. According to the scriptures, a redeemer delivers, saves, comforts, and restores (Psalm 37:40; 1 Nephi 10:6; Psalm 103:5; Isaiah 40:31). The problem is, whenever I felt stressed, anxious, or upset, I didn't turn to my true Redeemer to deliver me, I reached for some M&M's or cookie dough instead. In scriptural terms, I talked of chocolate, rejoiced in chocolate, and preached of chocolate (2 Nephi 25:26). It was my "refuge in times of trouble" (Psalm 9:9) and the "rejoicing of mine heart" (Jeremiah 15:16). The Lord finally made it clear that the only way I could be transformed was to turn my back on this counterfeit deliverer and put my trust in *Him*, my "Savior and . . . Redeemer, the Mighty One of Israel" (1 Nephi 22:12).[2]

There was another reason I needed to fast from my affection for chocolate. I discovered it in these simple words from the Apostle James: "But every man is tempted, when he is drawn away of his own lust, and enticed. Then when lust hath conceived, it bringeth forth sin: and sin, when it is finished, bringeth forth death" (James 1:14–15).

Now, I know this verse doesn't seem to have anything to do with food since it appears to be talking to those who struggle with sexual feelings of lust. But what if I told you that the original Greek word for *lust* in this verse is *epithymia*, which simply means "craving," "longing," or "strong desire of any kind"?[3] It gives the verse a much broader meaning, don't you think? With this definition in place, we can see that James isn't just referring to a lust for sex, but to our longing for *anything* that pleases and satisfies our flesh. When I began to look at the verse that way, I had to admit that chocolate was one of my most persistent fleshly cravings. Though I never called my craving "lust," that's exactly what it was. It was a "strong desire" that controlled me, an appetite that held me firmly in its clutches.

I want to be clear: I'm not saying that my eating of chocolate was sinful—it was my *lusting* after it. That's because every time I lusted after a candy bar (every time my strong desire flared up), I moved heaven and earth to satisfy that powerful craving. For this reason, the Apostle Peter counsels us, "Dearly beloved, I beseech you . . . abstain from fleshly lusts, which war against the soul" (1 Peter 2:11). Notice that Peter instructed us to *abstain*, to fast, to deny ourselves the fleshly lusts that war against our soul.

Perhaps you're wondering, "How in the world can a brownie or some M&M's war against your soul?" We can find the answer in Romans chapter 6. Believe it or not, Paul used the same Greek word for *lust* when he said, "Let not sin therefore reign in your mortal body, that ye should obey it in the lusts thereof" (Romans 6:12). Then he pointed out that every time I obeyed my lust—meaning every time I gave in to my body's powerful fleshly desires—I allowed those cravings to "reign" or have "dominion" over me (Romans 6:14). "Know ye not," Paul declared, "that to whom ye yield yourselves servants to obey, his servants ye are to whom ye obey?" (Romans 6:16). The Apostle's point is that by allowing my cravings to dominate my life, I'd become a servant of my flesh rather than a servant of God (Romans 6:17–18). It was quite a startling revelation but one I knew deep down in my soul to be true.[4]

With those two points established, the Spirit unveiled one final reason I needed to give up the chocolate. It was one of those "Duh!" moments when the Lord metaphorically took me by the shoulders, looked me square in the eyes, and said, *Jaci, think about it for a minute. Of course you're going to have body image issues if you overdose on sugar. Of course you're going to have problems with your weight if you eat the way you do. It all comes down to the fact that you're not taking care of yourself the way I've taught you in the Word of Wisdom. It's time for you to bury this particular sword and start a new life.*

He drove His point home by directing me to Daniel chapter 1. It seems I'd missed one particular lesson taught by Shadrach, Meshach, and Abed-nego. You see, before the three Hebrews were ever placed in positions of authority, and before they displayed the courage to turn from Nebuchadnezzar's golden idol, these faithful men proved that they knew how to abstain.

It happened when the trio first arrived in court with their friend Daniel. At the time, "the king appointed them a daily provision of the king's meat, and of the wine which he drank: so nourishing them three years, that at the end thereof they might stand before the king" (Daniel 1:5). Listen to the way Daniel responded to this particular situation:

> But Daniel purposed in his heart that he would not defile himself with the portion of the king's meat, nor with the wine which he drank: therefore he requested of the prince of the eunuchs that he might not defile himself. . . .
>
> Then said Daniel to Melzar, whom the prince of the eunuchs had set over Daniel, Hananiah, Mishael, and Azariah,
>
> Prove thy servants, I beseech thee, ten days; and let them give us pulse to eat, and water to drink.
>
> Then let our countenances be looked upon before thee, and the countenance of the children that eat of the portion of the king's meat: and as thou seest, deal with thy servants. (Daniel 1:8, 11–13)

With the eunuch's consent, the four friends fasted from the king's rich food and drink, subsisting instead on fare that echoes the very diet laid out in the Word of Wisdom. I'm referring to the "pulse," or the vegetables and grains, not just the absence of alcohol and the sparing use of meat. What happened at the end of ten days? The scriptures say their "countenances appeared fairer and fatter in flesh than all the children which did eat the portion of the king's meat" (Daniel 1:15). And notice this additional assessment:

As for these four children, God gave them knowledge and skill in all learning and wisdom: and Daniel had understanding in all visions and dreams. . . .

And the king communed with them; and among them all was found none like Daniel, Hananiah, Mishael, and Azariah. . . .

And in all matters of wisdom and understanding, that the king enquired of them, he found them ten times better than all the magicians and astrologers that were in all his realm. (Daniel 1:17, 19–20)

The lesson in these verses is powerful. Because of their fasting, the four Hebrews were not only the healthiest in the palace, they also enjoyed spiritual blessings far beyond any in the land. It just goes to show that there's a greater connection between the lusts of our flesh and our spiritual lives than we've ever imagined.

I don't share this story to say that we should all become vegetarians or start some new diet trend of only pulse and water, or even to suggest that everyone should give up chocolate. I share it to show how abstinence brings blessings that can come in no other way. That's because fasting changes our focus. It refines and purifies our desires. It starves the lusts of our flesh. Most important, it displays our commitment to follow Jesus Christ. Only through fasting can we receive a body image breakthrough. Only through fasting can we learn to think and live like a true daughter of God.

I need to tell you that even though we've worked our way through a great deal of the transformation process, there's still a huge barrier standing in our way. For this reason, we're going to carry our discussion on fasting into the next chapter. The problem with fasting is this: when it comes down to it, abstinence is *just plain hard*. It's not something our natural man enjoys doing. Our desires often work against us so we don't *want* to give up the lusts of our flesh. For instance, I saw a sign on an office wall once that said, "Deliver me from evil, but leave my chocolate alone!" That was exactly how I felt. My lusts tasted good to me. They satisfied me. The last thing I wanted to do was bury my favorite things in the earth and walk away.

So how in the world do we give up things we feel very attached to? How do we walk away when our desires are shouting at us to stay? Answers to those important questions are just a few short pages away.

For Additional Study

Read the account of the rich young ruler in Matthew 19:16–22. What did the Lord ask this young man to do? How can we relate this to the kind of fasting we've been talking about? Now turn to Doctrine and Covenants 25:10 and answer those same questions.

Look up Doctrine and Covenants 58:43 and Proverbs 28:13. What word in these verses correlate to the concept of fasting or abstinence? You might find it interesting that the word *forsake* actually means "to quit or leave entirely; abandon; desert; to give up or renounce."[5] Why do you think it's important to "abandon" or "give up" our lusts? What does the Lord promise in Proverbs 28:13 to one who not only confesses but also forsakes their sinful ways?

To continue to explore the word *forsake*, take a minute to read Matthew 19:29; Luke 14:33; and Alma 39:9. How do these verses clarify the things we've just discussed?

Returning to the account of the Anti-Nephi-Lehies, what was it that enabled the people to leave their swords buried in the earth? Why didn't they dig them back up (or even make new swords) when threatened with an invading Lamanite army? I believe the answer lies in Alma 19:33. How can this particular scripture apply to your efforts to abstain from the things of the world?

I want to be clear that this chapter certainly doesn't negate the power of actual fasting, where we abstain from food for a time to draw closer to the Lord. This practice can definitely be used to give us the spiritual power we need to abstain from other things in our lives. (See Alma 17:3 and Helaman 3:35.) Also, as we begin to apply the things we've just learned, we need to be careful not to confuse abstinence with starving ourselves or getting caught up in some sort of fad diet. Only the Lord can show us how to apply the concept of abstinence in a way that will lead us to healing and not further obsession and idolatry.

The Feast of Christ

atisfaction. It's a word that evokes a sense of peace, fullness, and contentment. If we're satisfied, our hunger is relieved, our desire is fulfilled, and our soul is completely at rest. This picture shows up in our home every fast Sunday. But it doesn't come without some difficulty along the way. At the moment, three of our sons are active, food-loving teenagers, which should explain why fasting is such a continual struggle at our house. As these boys fast each month, they constantly regale me with all the torturous side effects of their ravenous hunger. One complains about feeling light-headed, another can't get up off the couch, and still another grows irritable as the hours drag on. Clearly, my sons feel like they're starving to death. Their bodies are in desperate need of life-giving nourishment.

I love it when the moment finally arrives—the moment when our family sits down to a feast of steaming roast beef, creamy mashed potatoes, and perfectly seasoned gravy. My boys experience such joy in every bite, you'd think they'd died and gone to heaven. What I see at that dinner table is more than relief, more than just a pleasant Sunday meal. It's ecstasy. Absolute pleasure. The ultimate in bodily satisfaction.

I tell that story to illustrate the problem inherent in fasting: our bodies can only go without nourishment for so long. No matter how hard we try be strong, sooner or later, our hunger gets the best of us, and we're compelled to find a way to fill ourselves back up. The hard truth is that we can't live without satisfaction. It seems to be genetically tied to our body's strongest and most influential impulses.

What's more, we tend to forget that our physical body isn't the only part of us that longs to be satisfied. Our soul also has an appetite of its own (see Enos 1:4). Why does our soul hunger and thirst? I believe it again goes back to the Fall. Remember, because we've been cast out of our Father's presence and cut off from the tree of life, we're left with that inner hunger we talked about earlier, that emptiness we continually struggle to fill. Make no mistake, we long to satisfy our soul hunger the same way my boys yearn for food on fast Sunday. The problem is, we're not always aware that's what we're doing.

I spent years wondering why I used food for reasons other than true physical hunger. I watched myself eat when I was sad, bored, restless, or even for no reason at all. Most of the time, I simply concluded that I lacked the willpower to control my physical appetite. But eventually the Spirit showed me that I was using chocolate (and doughnuts and brownies and chocolate chip cookie dough) to fill my emptiness, satisfy my hungry soul, and give my heart the fulfillment it was searching for in this lost and fallen world. I'll admit that these little treats definitely soothed my soul's hunger in the short term. In fact, the experience was so gratifying, I couldn't help myself—I just kept going back for more.

It could be that you thought another pair of shoes would fill your void, even though your closet is already bursting at the seams. It could be you tried to calm your restlessness by getting more followers on social media, by attracting the attention of men, or by seeking popularity in the eyes of your peers. Often it's hard to see that we're using these things to help us cope with our soul hunger, that we're relying on them to fill the emptiness we feel inside as a result of the Fall.

Now, we just talked in the previous chapter about burying these escapes just like the Anti-Nephi-Lehies buried their swords. And perhaps, deep down, we know we need to give up our little obsessions; we know it will help us draw closer to God. But there's a huge problem with this type of fasting. It's that our fleshly lusts are our guilty pleasures or the things that bring us that rush of happiness and excitement from day to day. Because they've worked so well in feeding our hungry hearts over the years, the thought of living without them can make us feel like all our joy is being taken away. We may even want to stomp our foot and reply, "That's not fair! Can't I have any pleasure at all? Am I really supposed to live in a constant state of deprivation for the rest of my life?" We feel this way because fasting seems to leave our heart feeling so empty. Like there's nothing left to live for but some far distant eternal reward. If these feelings persist, we'll throw out all thoughts of abstinence and run right back to the thing that temporarily fills our hunger. In contrast to the Anti-Nephi-Lehies, we'll return to the place where we buried our swords and dig them up all over again.

In order to move forward, we must understand that we're not burying our favorite things only to metaphorically "starve" for the rest of our days. We're not putting off all gratification and pleasure only to remain in a state of perpetual emptiness. We're fasting from the lusts of our flesh for one reason and one reason only: so we can sit ourselves down at the incomparable, soul-filling, completely satisfying *feast of Christ*. In other words, we're abstaining from a lesser type of food *in order to partake of something better.* The good news is, it's a diet so sustaining, "[our] soul shall never hunger nor thirst, but shall be filled" (3 Nephi 20:8).

I want to clarify that when I refer to the feast of Christ, I'm not just talking about the warm, peaceful feeling we sometimes feel at church, or the simple joy that comes from reading our scriptures or worshipping in the temple. This feast entails much more than that. In reality, it's the most luscious, mouth-watering banquet you could ever imagine. If you've seen the movie *Hook*, picture the sumptuous feast the Lost Boys dreamt up in their game with Peter. It's a meal that offers *everlasting satisfaction* for your hungry soul. Jesus described this abundant feast in John chapter 6, but to truly understand His teachings, we need to go back to the beginning of this unusual and enlightening scriptural story.

The scene opens with a great, and hungry, multitude following after Christ. To address the crowd's hunger, the Lord turns to Philip and asks, "Whence shall we buy bread, that these may eat?" (John 6:5). Philip essentially shrugs his shoulders, so Andrew points out a boy with five barley loaves and two small fishes, but then comments, "What are they among so many?" (John 6:9). What, indeed? Christ then feeds five thousand people with this one simple meal and instructs His disciples to gather up what will eventually become twelve baskets of leftovers. This is no small miracle for a quiet little village in Galilee.

It's no wonder that the next day finds the multitude again clamoring after Jesus. As they entreat Him a second time, the Lord takes a very different approach than He did the day before when He says,

> Verily, verily, I say unto you, Ye seek me, not because ye saw the miracles, but because ye did eat of the loaves, and were filled. Labour not for the meat which perisheth, but for that meat which endureth unto everlasting life, which the Son of man shall give unto you (John 6:26–27).

It's as if Christ is telling the people, "You're only seeking me because you want your stomachs refilled. You want another temporary fix. But I have a kind of food to give you that you haven't even begun to understand. And there is nothing temporary about it." The Lord then reveals exactly what He's talking about with these staggering words: "I am the bread of life: he that cometh to me shall *never* hunger; and he that believeth on me shall *never* thirst" (verse 35; italics added).

Now, I don't want to pass this verse too quickly because there are a few points we absolutely must understand. First, notice how Jesus takes the time to acknowledge the people's persistent soul hunger, a hunger that can't be satisfied by loaves or fishes (or chocolate or social media or new shoes), which "perisheth." He then tells the Jews that what they really need is the "bread of life," a nourishment so miraculous, it will satiate their hunger so that it never returns.

If we apply this verse to our own lives, we'll hear Christ telling us that if we'll simply feast on *Him* rather than the things of the world, our soul will live in a state of *perpetual, unending satisfaction*. Feast on Him and there will be no more desperate yearnings, and no more emptiness and despair. In fact, the Lord has the power to "[prepare] a table" so full and inviting, and so laden with good things, we'll watch in awe as our cup "runneth over" (Psalm 23:5).

Let me share a little analogy to illustrate why fasting from the lusts of our flesh is such an important step in the transformation process. Imagine for a minute that you live in a land of castles and kings, and that you've received an invitation to attend a formal banquet in honor of the prince. Before leaving the house, you take a minute to fill your purse with a couple of Twinkies, half a box of Ding Dongs, and a few small bags of M&M's. Then you set off to experience what is sure to be the feast of a lifetime. (Yes, I know Ding Dongs and Twinkies don't fit in a story about castles and kings, but I'm hoping you'll humor me.)

Once you're seated in the king's grand hall, you watch wide-eyed as dish after sumptuous dish is brought out and placed on the table before you. But at the very moment your hunger promises to be utterly and completely fulfilled, your thoughts revert to the tempting treats you previously tucked into the confines of your purse. Without stopping to think about what you're doing, you unsnap your bag and grab the first Ding Dong your fumbling fingers can reach. In a matter of seconds, the wrapper is discarded and the taste of the chocolate explodes on the tip of your tongue. The satisfaction is so fulfilling that you reach for a Twinkie next, and then a bag of M&M's. At last, the rumbling in your stomach begins to subside. You're so caught up in the pleasure of your treats that it takes several minutes to realize that the other guests are devouring the king's extravagant banquet without you. Embarrassed, you quickly fill your plate and mouth, only to find that the food isn't as satisfying as you thought it would be. You travel home feeling like you missed something significant, only you're not even sure what it could be.

I'm sure you can see the connection to our lives today. Each of us has been invited to an extraordinary banquet unlike anything we've ever imagined. It's a celebration so bountiful and abundant, we've been promised we can "feast . . . even until [we] are filled" (Alma 32:42). But rather than giving this meal our full attention, many of us leave that exquisite food sitting on the table and rely instead on different types of junk food to feed our hungry soul. In order to continue the transformation process, we must now make a very important decision.

If you really, truly want to partake of the feast of Christ—meaning you really, truly want to be healed of the body image issues that stress your soul and torment your mind—then you have to set down your metaphorical Twinkies once and for all. Like the Anti-Nephi-Lehies, you've got to bury your fleshly lusts deep in the earth and walk away. Only by freeing yourself from these distractions can you finally partake in all that the Lord's delicious banquet has to offer.

I know it probably seems like an enormous sacrifice to let go of your most comforting escapes. Like I said, they've tasted pretty good to your soul over the years, which is why you've continued to turn to them again and again. But let me remind you, again, that what you're doing is laying down all your *short-term* comforts in order to partake of a feast that boasts a number of astonishing, *long-term* blessings. We'll find some of these blessings listed in one of the most beautiful passages of scripture on fasting. As you absorb these words from Isaiah, I want you to imagine the soul-satisfying feast you will receive if you'll find the courage to bury your swords and start a new life:

> Is not this the fast that I have chosen? to . . . undo the heavy burdens, and to let the oppressed go free, and that ye break every yoke?
>
> . . . Then shall thy light break forth as the morning, and thine health shall spring forth speedily: and thy righteousness shall go before thee; the glory of the Lord shall be thy rearward.
>
> Then shalt thou call, and the Lord shall answer; thou shalt cry, and he shall say, Here I am. . . . [T]hen shall thy light rise in obscurity, and thy darkness be as the noonday:
>
> And the Lord shall guide thee continually, and satisfy thy soul in drought, and make fat thy bones: and thou shalt be like a watered garden, and like a spring of water, whose waters fail not (Isaiah 58:6, 8–11).

Would you like to see your "heavy burdens" undone and the "yoke" of the image broken? Would you like your health to "spring forth speedily" and the Lord to "guide you continually"? Would you like your Savior to "satisfy [your] soul in drought, and make fat

[your] bones"? Would you enjoy becoming a "watered garden, . . . whose waters fail not"? It really is possible—if you'll fast from the lusts of your flesh, if you'll abstain from all the lies and propaganda coming from the great and spacious building. In other words, it's time to destroy your graven images, to break them in pieces and cut them down. Only then can you savor every single bite of your Lord's magnificent feast. Only then can your soul hunger be completely and everlastingly fulfilled.

Before we move on, let's quickly review the steps we've covered so far in the transformation process. First, we looked for false beliefs hidden deep inside our mind. As part of this process, we asked the Lord to search our heart, we confessed our sins, and we sought our Savior's enabling grace. Then we committed to fast from anything that's distracting us or causing us to sin. So our goal for the next few chapters is to sit ourselves down at the feast of Christ and let Him overflow our plate with *truth*. I promise you, the results of this banquet will be extraordinary. At last, you'll know a beauty that's beyond compare.

For Additional Study

Read through these verses that describe additional blessings that will come as we lay down the worldly junk food and instead fill our souls with the extravagant feast of Christ (all italics added):

My God hath been my support; he hath *led me through mine afflictions* in the wilderness; and he hath *preserved m*e upon the waters of the great deep.

He hath *filled me with his love, even unto the consuming of my flesh.*

He hath *confounded mine enemies*, unto the causing of them to quake before me.

Behold, he hath *heard my cry* by day, and he hath *given me knowledge* by visions in the night-time.

And by day have I waxed bold in mighty prayer before him; yea, my voice have I sent up on high; and angels came down and ministered unto me.

And upon the wings of his Spirit hath my body been carried away upon exceedingly high mountains. And *mine eyes have beheld great things*, yea, even too great for man; therefore I was bidden that I should not write them. (2 Nephi 4:21–25)

And it came to pass that I did go forth and partake of the fruit thereof; and I beheld that it was most sweet, above all that I ever before tasted. And as I partook of the fruit thereof it *filled my soul with exceedingly great joy*; wherefore, . . . I knew that it was desirable above all other fruit. (1 Nephi 8:11)

And they all cried with one voice, saying: Yea, . . . the Spirit of the Lord Omnipotent, . . .as *wrought a mighty change in us, or in our hearts*, that we have *no more disposition to do evil, but to do good continually.* (Mosiah 5:2)

And it came to pass that I, Nephi, beheld the *power of the Lamb of God, that it descended upon the saints of the church of the Lamb, and upon the covenant people of the Lord,* who were scattered upon all the face of the earth; and they were *armed with righteousness and with the power of God in great glory.* (1 Nephi 14:14)

Once again, I want you to consider what you would give to receive such life-altering blessings. What would you be willing to bury deep in the earth? In Alma 22:15 and 18, King Lamoni's father explains the sacrifice he is willing to make. How do you think his words could apply to your battle with body image?

Beauty for Ashes

n 2008 our family watched with joy as a temple was constructed in our hometown of Rexburg, Idaho. As fun as it was to see the magnificent edifice rise from the dust, nothing matched the excitement of the open house and dedication. The dedication was so profoundly sacred, I can hardly find words to describe it. The blessing of having a temple in our midst lit up the hearts of both young and old.

I think my favorite part of the whole experience came during the open house when Greg and I had the privilege of leading tour groups through the temple. During these tours, we'd share details of the temple's construction and the intricate beauty of the house of the Lord. As we walked the hallowed halls, we'd point out the murals that took two years to paint, the rich wood imported from Africa, and the handcrafted stained glass windows with the representation of a wheat stalk. It didn't take long for me to realize that I wasn't just leading tourists through an impressive structure, I was leading them through the house of God.

I'll confess that something happened to me during those four weeks of leading tours. The building became more than just a temple; it became my second home. It felt personal. It felt comfortable and even familiar. My heart grew deeply attached to that wonderful place. It's an attachment I still feel even though it's been several years since our temple was dedicated. Like my own home, the temple is one of my very favorite places to be.

Now read the words of another who loved the temple, the Psalmist David. Although in his day the structure looked very different, David's adoration and love for this sacred place warms my heart like a soft ray of light.

> One thing have I desired of the Lord, that will I seek after; that I may dwell in the house of the Lord all the days of my life, to behold the beauty of the Lord, and to inquire in his temple (Psalm 27:4).

Did you notice what David found in the temple? It's something that applies very much to our current discussion. He noticed the rare and wonderful "beauty of the Lord." It's a beauty far removed from that of the world. But this beauty is very real, and it's the very thing our hearts have been searching for all along.

I'd like to examine the connection between the temple and the beauty of the Lord. Through the temple, we'll learn more about the beauty that will begin to reside in us throughout the transformation process. The best part is, the closer we draw to Christ, and the further we draw from our false beliefs and the polluting noise of the image, we won't have to strive or clamor for this precious beauty—it will simply fill us, "distil[ling] on [our] soul as the dews from heaven" (D&C 121:45). Slowly and sweetly, the beauty of the Lord will be "engraven on [our] countenances" (Alma 5:19). It will be a natural byproduct of partaking of the magnificent feast of the Lord.

First, I'd like to show you some pictures of temples from around the world. As you look at the following photos, take a minute to think about what you see.

I'm hoping you noticed the uniqueness of each structure, and the vast differences in building materials, architecture, and design. It doesn't take long to realize that no two temples are exactly alike. Instead, each one possesses its own individual look, often reflecting the culture and ethnicity of the land in which it resides. This one characteristic teaches us a great deal about the beauty of the Lord.

Remember, when the Savior commanded His people to build temples in this dispensation, He could have revealed one master design, one look He believed to be more beautiful than all the rest. "This is it," He could have said, "the ultimate in beauty. I want every single temple to look *just like this.*" Then, no matter where in the world a temple arose, it would have been built according to the exact same specifications: same size; same exterior; same carpet; same lighting fixtures; same woodwork, landscaping, and trim. To be sure, the results of this plan would have been very beautiful, but also very boring. Who wants a bunch of cookie-cutter buildings dotting the earth? If you've seen one temple, you've seen them all. It would definitely have taken the magic out of our magnificent, awe-inspiring temples.

And yet, isn't that exactly how the world teaches us to measure a woman's beauty? There's one image, one look that everyone must match. This image makes no allowances for genetics, ethnicity, or personal preference, but instead it presents a master plan of conformity, a one-size-fits-all standard that's both fictitious and shallow. Do you see how that in no way reflects the true beauty of the Lord? For another example, take a look at the earth around you. You'll find not a cookie-cutter plan but an incredible amount of diversity in God's creations. Rather than boasting one look, one climate, or one landscape, each part of the world possesses its own unique and individual beauty. Some lands feature tropical beaches or lush foliage while others sport rugged mountains or rushing streams. Just like the diversity found in our temples, the earth stands as a witness that our Redeemer treasures beauty in many different shapes and forms.

That's why it's so important for you allow the Lord to show you your *own* unique beauty. Your eye color, skin tone, hair texture, and body shape are part of what makes you, you. Comparing yourself to someone else is like comparing the Salt Lake Temple to the temple in Washington, D.C. You just can't do it. Each temple is constructed exactly the way it was supposed to be. Just like a temple, your distinctive characteristics were meant to reflect an exquisite radiance all your own.

Now, I'll admit that it may take some time for us to really believe deep in our hearts that we're beautiful. After all, many of us have spent decades loathing our bodies—or at least certain parts of it. Thankfully, the Lord holds the power to resurrect the way we see ourselves and bring our beauty back to life. But in order for this to happen, we must be "renewed in the spirit of [our] mind[s]" so we see our bodies through His eyes rather than the mocking voices of the world (Ephesians 4:23). Thus, our most important goal, after turning away from the image, is to spend time asking Him to teach us new ways to think and feel about our physical bodies. In a word, we need revelation. We need to replace the lies in our heads with enduring, soul-restoring truth.

As I asked the Lord to fill my mind with truth, He surprised me by zeroing in on something I've already mentioned—my attachment to long hair. Now, there's absolutely nothing wrong with having long hair. It's one of the most beautiful features a woman can enjoy. The problem was that I was using the length of my hair to measure my identity and worth. It seems my Savior was ready to show me that my worth went much deeper than what was growing out of the top of my head.

He did this by orchestrating a situation I'd already experienced before. You guessed it—I ended up with another terrible haircut. I'm not sure if the stylist was just having a bad day or what, but she left the length of my hair much longer on one side than on the other. My only recourse was to find another stylist to fix it, and once she did, I again found myself staring in the mirror at a head of much-dreaded short hair. The reason I say the Lord orchestrated this situation is because, after looking at the devastating change in my appearance, I felt Him say, *Jaci, it's time to let go of all your restricting beliefs about yourself and let me rework the way you see your beauty. Let me show you what can happen when you surrender your appearance into My hands.* What happened after that was nothing short of miraculous.

Once I eased my grip on my own preconceived ideas, the Lord began to teach me how to see my appearance solely through His eyes. Soon I realized that this new, shorter cut worked well with my facial structure, was easier to fix, and better fit my daily routine. It's a style I'd never considered because of the limiting beliefs I held about my hair. In the end, I decided it felt fresh, updated, and even pretty. As my old beliefs slowly melted away, I finally understood that the Lord was interested not in my new haircut but in helping me *move beyond the lies to a better place.* Little did I know, He was only getting started in my personal transformation.

The next area He highlighted was that horror of all horrors—the department store fitting room. I'll admit that, for me, it was not a fun place to be. More often than not, I entered the dressing room with an armful of clothes that seemed darling on the hanger, but then I ended up handing every single piece right back to the attendant when I was through. Nothing ever seemed to fit right, or when it did, the item often didn't fit my budget. On a good shopping day, I'd spend hours only to find maybe one thing I liked. It was not a pleasant experience.

I'll sheepishly admit that I never even considered praying for help with this particular dilemma. It seems I'd put the Lord in a spiritual box and kept Him there. I'd always assumed He was only interested in my obedience to His commandments. Thankfully, He was ready to show me that He was interested in *every* facet of my life, including the areas that I labeled worldly or temporal. Let me describe one shopping trip that put a smile on my face for the rest of the day.

The goal of this trip was simple: I needed something new to wear to church. Since I'd already found some brown heels on sale, the thought crossed my mind that it might be fun to look for something pink and brown, one of my favorite color combinations. I said a quiet prayer with the intent of bringing the Spirit with me as my companion as I shopped. I kid you not, within about thirty minutes of starting my shopping, I found myself standing in a dressing room wearing the cutest pink and brown skirt set I'd ever laid eyes on. It fit perfectly, not just on my body, but also in my budget. To say I was astounded would be an enormous under-statement. At that moment, I felt the Lord say, *Jaci, you were never meant to endure this life alone. I want to help you see yourself through My eyes. I want to show you who you really are.*

Suddenly, that little fitting room resembled a temple as I felt wrapped in my Savior's intimate tenderness and all-encompassing love. I couldn't believe the personal care He'd offered me, especially in an area that had caused me so much stress and anxiety. Right then and there, I surrendered myself into His loving arms, wanting nothing more than to "render to him" all that I was and all that I would ever become (Mosiah 2:34). If we allow the Lord to help us adorn our physical bodies, I promise He will work miracles in our lives, even if money is tight and opportunities are few.

However, in sharing these personal examples, please don't think I'm saying that everyone needs to get a new haircut or go shopping in order to feel beautiful. That's not my point at all. I recognize that each of us struggles with different issues, issues that may have nothing to do with hair or the stressful experience in the fitting room. What I *am* suggesting is that, whatever your issues are, you allow Christ to help you care for and beautify your physical body. I promise you, if you'll turn your appearance over to Him, He'll make much more of it than you ever could. He'll erase your insecurities and show you how to find a look that makes you feel happy and content. All you need to do is give Him a chance.

It's important to remember that the Lord isn't interested in helping us look more like the image. He's not going to make us a size 6 if that's not the size our bodies were meant to be. Instead, His goal is to help us embrace our own unique beauty and individual style. For instance, some of us love bright colors while others prefer subdued tones; some choose high heels while others like flats; some enjoy wearing makeup while others are content to let their natural beauty shine from within. That's the wonderful thing about the beauty of the Lord—we each get to choose the look that we're most comfortable with. Our Savior is willing to help us with this because He knows our greatest happiness will come not by forming ourselves to the image but in rejoicing in who we are as individual daughters of God.

At this point, I know there are those who may be thinking, "I have bigger problems than my hair or the drama in the fitting room. I just lost my both of my breasts to cancer," or "My body is struggling with the effects of multiple sclerosis," or "I'm a middle-aged woman who's way past her prime. I don't think I'll *ever* feel comfortable with the way I look." Here's where the good news of Christ goes beyond *good* to *absolutely incredible*. I'll let Isaiah have the honor of revealing some amazing promises, promises that hold the key to all the despair and hopelessness we feel as a result of our mortal bodies. Speaking messianically, the prophet writes,

> The Spirit of the Lord God is upon me; because the Lord hath anointed me to . . . bind up the brokenhearted, . . . to comfort all that mourn;
> To appoint unto them that mourn in Zion, to give unto them beauty for ashes, the oil of joy for mourning, the garment of praise for the spirit of heaviness; that they might be called trees of righteousness, the planting of the Lord, that he might be glorified. (Isaiah 61:1–3)

Truly, these are beautiful and inspiring words. We're told that Christ can bind up the brokenhearted, comfort those that mourn,

and give beauty for ashes. Notice: *beauty* for ashes. I know we sometimes assume that these promises refer mainly to the blessings of the
resurrection, but I believe Isaiah was talking about much more than
that. I believe the Lord holds the power to restore and renew us even
while we're living in mortality, even amid all our weaknesses and ailments, and even if our appearance doesn't look the way we think it
should. No matter what we're asked to suffer physically, the Lord's
Atonement can address all the guilt, shame, and pain found in the
difficult trials that come with having a mortal body.

I learned this lesson one fall as I prepared to join my husband at
a conference in southern California. It was to be a joint LDS-Evan-
gelical meeting of the minds, a weekend for Mormons and other
Christians to come together with the hope of building new bridges of
friendship and understanding. I was really looking forward to meeting new people and discussing our common love of Jesus Christ.

However, something distressing happened a few days before
we were scheduled to leave. I developed one of those hormonal
cysts I mentioned earlier right in the middle of my cheek. In fact,
the cyst was so large, the physician's assistant friend I went to
for treatment did a double take when I walked in the door. "You
weren't kidding about needing to see me," he said. To my dismay,
even after receiving an injection, the ulcer took its sweet time healing, and I was forced to attend the conference with what looked
like a swollen, purple boil on my face.

As I pondered the situation on the plane ride to California,
the phrase "beauty for ashes" came to my mind again and again.
I remembered that the "sting of death is swallowed up in Christ"
(Mosiah 16:8), but I wondered how that could apply to my current
situation. It was then that I felt the Lord say, *Jaci, it's not just the
sting of your actual physical death that's swallowed up in Me. It's also
all the side effects of being mortal—all the aging, illness, deformity,
disease, weakness, and shame. Remember, Alma said that I'll take upon
Me all the pains and sicknesses of My people (Alma 7:11). That means I
can even help you with the shame of a big cyst on your face.*

To prove His point, I watched in awe as He worked a small
miracle over the next few days. No, the cyst didn't magically disap-
pear the moment I stepped off the airplane. Instead, what happened

is that I basically forgot all about it. As I met new people and spent time in conversation, all my shame in my appearance quickly faded away. The cyst just wasn't that big of a deal anymore. I was at peace, content to accept the fact that physical suffering is part of life and it was my turn to experience a little of it. Losing our shame is another wonderful benefit that comes from sitting down at the banquet table and partaking of the glorious feast of Christ.

Now, I know my story doesn't even begin to compare with some of the more agonizing trials we experience, like painful diseases or crippling disabilities. But I believe with all my heart that the lesson is the same. When it comes to our outward appearance, I know that *all* our "afflictions" can be "swallowed up in the joy of Christ" (Alma 31:38). No matter what we're forced to deal with, His power is strong enough to carry the burden. But the only way our embarrassment and shame can fade away is for us to learn to trust Him, to "offer [our] whole souls as an offering unto him" (Omni 1:26). As He teaches us—through prayer and pondering and time spent with Him—to see ourselves the way He sees us, we'll soon view our bodies very differently, not because our appearance has been altered or our trials have disappeared but because our inward thoughts and feelings have dramatically changed.

Ultimately, what Jesus Christ is offering us is *rest*—rest from the pressure to conform to the image, rest from our insecurities and fears, and rest from the lies that have run rampant in our heads. To be at rest is to be free of anxiety, to be at peace both body and spirit. Moroni tells us that the "rest of the Lord" is something we can enjoy *"from this time henceforth* until [we] shall rest with him in heaven" (Moroni 7:3; italics added). It's a rest obtained not by reaching our goal weight or by fitting ourselves to the image but by finally embracing who we are as women of Christ.

Authors John and Stasi Eldredge illustrate this point by describing two very different women. Notice how each one expresses her own individual beauty:

> Janet is twenty-one. She was on the dance team in high school. Small and petite with a fabulous figure. Unlike so many women in that world of competitive beauty, she escaped an eating disorder. But she runs between five and ten miles *a day*. She watches what

she eats. She's able to wear the cutest clothes. And yet . . . when you're with her, your heart does not rest. Her beauty impresses, but it does not invite. The reason is simple: She is striving. She is a perfectionist. . . . Her beauty feels tenuous, shaky. It is not flowing from her heart. It's almost as if it's forced, from the outside, through discipline and fear.

June is one of the most beautiful women we have ever met. . . . Her hair was long, swept up loosely and held by decorative combs. She wore unique, dangly earrings and pretty flowing skirts. Her eyes sparkled when she laughed, which she did often, and her smile lit up the room. . . . June was at rest with herself, at home in who she was. Talking with her, just being with her, made us feel more at rest with ourselves as well. Her spacious, beautiful soul invited others to come, to be, to taste and see that the Lord is good. . . . And June was seventy-five years old.

What is the difference between these two women? Rest. June's beauty flows from a heart at rest.[1]

In the Eldredges' description of June, we find a perfect picture of a woman filled with the beauty of the Lord. She's a women who's "at rest with herself" and "at home in who she [is]." Notice that for June, being at rest didn't mean she gave no thought to physical attractiveness. Instead, she embraced her own style, a style that reflected her distinct personality and uniqueness. For June, that meant dangly earrings, flowing skirts, and decorative combs. For you, it may include a French manicure, some classy jewelry to accent your outfit, or touching up your hair with a fresh dose of highlights. Though in the past you may have turned to those things as a way of covering your insecurities or imitating the worldly image of beauty, once you embark in the transformation process, you'll view these things as a way of *delighting* in your physical body and *rejoicing* in the wondrous gift you've been given. Filled with the beauty of the Lord, you'll still take the time to adorn and beautify your physical body, but you'll no longer be caught up in the radical, obsessive, self-absorbed tendencies of the world. It's a wonderful place for our hearts and minds to live.

With that said, I'll happily tell you that there's much more to discover when it comes to the precious beauty of the Lord. I hope that by now your heart is beginning to pray with David: "let the beauty of the Lord our God be upon [me]" (Psalm 90:17), for "the Lord taketh pleasure in his people: he will beautify the meek with salvation" (Psalm 149:4).

For Additional Study

In the movie *Chronicles of Narnia: Voyage of the Dawn Treader*, Aslan chides Lucy for wanting to look like her older sister, Susan. After finding that Lucy has cast a spell to change her appearance, the Great Lion tells the girl, "You wished yourself away, and much more. You doubt your value. *Don't run from who you are.*" Could it be time to hear Christ speak the same words to your weary heart?

In the Book of Mormon we're told that the righteous "did not wear costly apparel, yet they were neat and comely" (Alma 1:27). While it's common knowledge that neatness implies orderliness and cleanliness,[2] we often forget that the word *comely* means "pleasing in appearance" or "attractive."[3] In fact, synonyms for *comely* include beautiful, stunning, graceful, pretty, and appealing.[4] So, when it comes to the way we adorn our physical bodies, take some time to ponder how we can follow this scriptural counsel without molding ourselves to fit the worldly image of beauty.

It's important to know that although we may have experienced a body image breakthrough, that doesn't mean our new feelings won't be put to the test. Satan will still try to tempt us to return to old ways of thinking and feeling. To help us withstand this temptation, let's review Ephesians 6: 10–18 and how it applies to our new and improved body image. For example,

- How do you "girt [your loins] with truth" about your body?
- How do you make sure your "feet [are] shod with the preparation of the gospel of peace"?
- How do you use "the sword of the Spirit" to help you slice through the enemy's lies regarding your appearance?
- How does "the shield of faith" help to "quench" the message of the image?
- In what ways can you "[watch] thereunto with all perseverance" over your new, positive body image?

Between Two Extremes

Have you ever read Peter's thoughts on a woman's true beauty? It's a subject the Apostle addresses in his first epistle. Here's what he had to say:

> [Let not your adorning] be that outward adorning of plaiting the hair, and of wearing of gold, or of putting on of apparel;
>
> But let it be the hidden man of the heart, in that which is not corruptible, even the ornament of a meek and quiet spirit, which is in the sight of God of great price. (1 Peter 3:3–4)

Wonderful words, but they raise a very important question. Isn't Peter contradicting all that talk in the last chapter about seeing our appearance in a whole new light? After all, he makes it quite clear that our focus shouldn't be on our "outward adorning" but on the "hidden man of the heart." Maybe rather than praying for help to see our own individual beauty, the best thing we could do is forget about our looks altogether. I mean, isn't Peter telling us we'll be more spiritual if we quit fussing over our hair or what we wear to church? I believe the best way to understand the Apostle's intent is to look again to the pattern of the temple.

If you consider all the critical ordinances that take place in the house of the Lord, it's obvious that the most important part of that sacred structure is what goes on inside. Echoing Peter's words, if all we ever do is walk around the grounds, admire the flowers, or take pictures of the outside, we've missed the whole point of going to the temple. Only inside can we make life-changing covenants.

Only inside can we be sealed to our families. Only inside can we be invited into the very presence of God.

And the same thing holds true for each of us, for we know the Lord looks not on our "outward appearance," but "on [our] heart" (1 Samuel 16:7). So as we continue the transformation process, it's crucial that we follow Peter's advice and ornament ourselves with a "meek and quiet spirit, which is in the sight of God of great price." But as we work to attain this level of spiritual beauty and maturity, does that mean we'll eventually reach a point where we no longer worry about the way we look? That's certainly not how the Lord handles the exterior of His temples. Remember, even though the inside of the temple is the most significant part, the Church still devotes a great deal of time to beautifying the grounds of each building. Precious tithing dollars are spent not only on exquisite furnishings for the inside but on elegant landscaping and materials for the outside. From this we can conclude that the Lord wants His houses to look attractive both inside *and* out. I believe He has a very important reason for making the exterior a priority.

The outside of the temple actually has a very powerful impact on all who see it or visit the grounds. Didn't you grow up admiring the outward beauty of the temple and dreaming of the day you could enter? To observers, the structure seems like a magical palace, a fairy-tale castle overflowing with the Spirit of the Lord. Consider how the temple's spires point upward and send our gaze drifting up to heaven. Contemplate the feelings of wonder and awe that come just by standing in the shadow of that glorious building. In the end, the outside of the temple does more than just look beautiful—it bears witness of the greatness and splendor of the Lord Jesus Christ. Even the very walls and windows speak of His goodness, His majesty, and His all-encompassing love.

I found it interesting that, in July 2011, the New Era printed a story about a group of Young Women who walked twenty-two miles from the Draper Temple to the Salt Lake City Temple. The amazing thing about this story is that these girls never even set foot inside either temple. Truth is, they didn't have to. The New Era reported that as "all of the 70 walkers gathered together on the steps of the Salt Lake Temple, . . . [they] held hands, embraced one another, and cried tears of joy."[1] Just being outside was incredibly powerful. It was enough to remind the girls of the happiness they'll experience as they grow closer to their precious Savior.

With that story in mind, read the words of Paul in his letter to the Corinthians:

> What? know ye not that your body is the temple of the Holy Ghost which is in you, which ye have of God, and ye are not your own?
>
> For ye are bought with a price: therefore glorify God *in your body, and in your spirit*, which are God's (1 Corinthians 6:19–20; italics added).

Do you see the parallel in these verses? We too are temples, and as such Paul says we're to use our bodies *and* our spirits to "glorify God." Why is this an important distinction? Elder David A. Bednar explains it this way: "Like it or not, other people make judgments about the restored gospel by what they see or feel in you and me."[2] In other words, before others ever encounter the beauty of our hearts, before they ever see the person we are on the inside, they first notice our bodies: how we care for them, dress them, and adorn them. That's why we can't ignore our looks as inconsequential. In the end, it's our outside and our inside *put together* that truly testify of Christ.

We've already talked about the woman who uses her looks to glorify herself rather than the Lord. It's the woman I believe Peter was talking about in his epistle. Her body resembles a Las Vegas casino more than a holy temple. Just like a casino's neon signs and glittering lights demand attention, this woman dresses and acts in a way to win the approval of the world. She is "lifted up in the pride of [her heart] . . . because of the costliness [or trendiness] of [her] apparel" (Jacob 2:13). She is obsessed with maintaining a look that those around her will praise and admire.

While we've discussed the dangers of becoming such a woman, what we haven't talked about yet is the other extreme. If one side of the coin is obsession with our looks, then the other side involves a complete disregard for our physical bodies. I believe *both* extremes cause harm, not only to ourselves but to the Lord whose representatives we are.

When we first think of neglecting our bodies, we may picture a woman who totally lets herself go, who takes no thought to care for or improve her outward appearance. She may rationalize her neglect with the thought that her husband should love her no matter what she looks like, or that she has no time for such things, or that her efforts are devoted to more noble pursuits than her looks. I'd like to suggest that these rationalizations in no way reflect the true beauty of the Lord.

My point is that we can't simply neglect our appearance with the rationalization that we're focusing instead on the development of our spirits. As a temple of God, our physical bodies need the same care and dedication the Church gives to the exterior of the houses of the Lord. Both the scriptures and modern prophets have given us a great deal of instruction on the importance of caring for our physical bodies. To illustrate, I'd like to focus on one set of instructions that many of us willfully disregard: the counsel on what we should eat.

I'm sure you'd agree that much of the food we take into our bodies looks nothing like the pure nourishment emphasized in the Word of Wisdom. We all know that soda, sugar, and junk food does nothing to meet our bodies' nutritional needs, but instead they leave us with a sluggish metabolism and a spreading waistline. Please know that I'm not saying these things in a spirit of judgment or condemnation. If I did, I'd be a hypocrite, since I've already talked about the horrible diet I lived on for most of my life. The reason I bring up this kind of neglect is because I never saw the way I ate as disrespect or disdain for my personal temple. I justified my actions by telling myself that it's what's on the inside that counts. But in reality, my food choices were having a crippling effect on what Peter called the "hidden man of [my] heart."

Yes, you heard me right. I believe the diet we feed our bodies has a dramatic effect on the state of our spirits. For starters, consider this story from former Young Women General President Susan W. Tanner:

> The restored gospel teaches that there is an intimate link between body, mind, and spirit. . . . I remember an incident in my home growing up when my mother's sensitive spirit was affected by a

physical indulgence. She had experimented with a new sweet roll recipe. They were big and rich and yummy—and very filling. Even my teenage brothers couldn't eat more than one. That night at family prayer my father called upon Mom to pray. She buried her head and didn't respond. He gently prodded her, "Is something wrong?" Finally she said, "I don't feel very spiritual tonight. I just ate three of those rich sweet rolls." I suppose that many of us have similarly offended our spirits at times by physical indulgences. . . . None of us can ignore this connection of our spirits and bodies.[3]

We may think indulging in junk food isn't doing any harm to our spirits, but it is. It goes back to the lesson we learned from Shadrach, Meshach, and Abed-nego. Only by fasting from Nebuchadnezzar's rich food and drink did these men become powerful "in all matters of wisdom and understanding" (Daniel 1:20). By abstaining in this way, they obtained the spiritual strength needed to withstand the allure of the golden image. Let me share how I learned this particular lesson for myself. As I continued to ask the Lord to fill my mind with truth, He chose to direct a giant spotlight on my out-of-control diet. Since I'd made such a mess of that part of my life, binging on sugar and then jumping from one diet to another in an attempt to lose weight, the first thing He did was put a book in my hands that radically changed everything I thought I knew about food and nutrition. The author was Kathleen DesMaisons, and the book was *The Sugar Addict's Total Recovery Program.*

Now, I'll admit that this wasn't the first time I'd come across this particular book. A few years earlier, I'd checked it out from the library only to dismiss the program as restrictive and unrealistic. (Of course, at the time, I was still living in deep denial of my sugar addiction.) But when a friend recommended the very same book the day after I'd offered a deeply personal and heartfelt prayer, I knew the Lord was telling me to take a hard look at the way I was feeding my body.

Just in case you're a fellow chocoholic who's also rationalizing your heavy intake of sweets, consider these questions Dr. DesMaisons poses to help her readers determine if sugar has moved beyond a simple treat to become an actual addiction in their everyday lives:

- Have you ever tried to cut down or control your use of sweet foods?
- Are you using more sweet foods than ever before?
- If you don't have your regular "dose" of sugar, do you get irritable and cranky? Have you ever gotten upset when someone ate your special food?
- Have you ever lied about how much sweet food you eat?
- Have you ever gone out of your way to get something sweet?
- Have you ever binged on sweet or white flour foods?
- Is it impossible to "just say no" to sweet foods?
- Is sugar controlling your life?[4]

Believe it or not, those are the very same questions used to evaluate alcoholics and other substance abusers. To my horror, almost every single question applied to me. It wasn't an easy thing to admit. I finally realized that my love for sugar wasn't just a bad habit or an unhealthy food choice, but it was an all-out addiction that held me firmly in its clutches.

At that moment, two powerful thoughts came to me. First was the fact that I'd spent my entire life looking down my nose at drug addicts and chain smokers when, in reality, I was just as hooked on a substance as they were. Second, even though I'd justified my chocolate habit with the excuse that it didn't keep me out of the temple like smoking or alcohol, the truth is that my addiction still kept me from enjoying the true feast of the Lord.

To prove my point, let me show you how our Savior feels about our use of food. Do you remember the passage in Doctrine and Covenants section 59 where He tells us that the purpose of food is to "gladden the heart" and "enliven the soul"? Well now pay attention to what He says in the very next verse:

> And it pleaseth God that he hath given all these things unto man; for unto this end were they made to be used, with judgment, not to excess, neither by extortion. (D&C 59:20)

Notice that the Lord tells us not to use food "to *excess*, neither by *extortion*." At first, it was easy for me to see how the "excess" part fit my sugar habit, but I wasn't sure how to interpret the "extortion" part until I found the following quote from Sister Tanner. Referring to this scripture, she said,

> My husband [taught] . . . that the "word extortion . . . literally means to 'twist out [or against].' Our use of . . . the body must not be twisted [against] the divinely ordained purposes for which [it was] given. *Physical pleasure is good in its proper time and place, but even then it must not become our god.*"[5]

With that I knew it was time to turn from this false god and tame the raging addiction that had taken over both my body and my life.

As I began to work my way through Dr. DesMaisons's book, one of the first things I learned was that my high intake of sugar was actually causing a chemical imbalance in my brain. In fact, this imbalance was so severe that it left me powerless against my body's sugar cravings. If that wasn't enough, Dr. DesMaisons also revealed a number of other symptoms that were directly tied to my high-sugar diet, things like depression, irritability, mood swings, fatigue, restlessness, feeling isolated and overwhelmed, and an inability to control my impulses. The crazy thing is, I'd definitely experienced all of those things, but I'd always blamed them on my stressful life, not on the chocolate I was downing by the pound. Finally I understood what a dramatic impact my diet was having not only on my weight but also on my emotions, moods, thoughts, willpower, and energy level.[6]

Over the next several months I relied heavily on the Lord to help me follow Dr. DesMaisons's gentle but powerful approach. Slowly and patiently, I learned to eat in a way that stabilized my brain chemicals and quieted my nagging sugar cravings once and for all. I won't lie, at first it was extremely difficult to stick with the program. Often it felt like I was taking one step forward and two steps back. But eventually, the power of my addiction lost its hold on me. I want to be very clear that even though Dr. DesMaisons's program held the truths I needed to overcome my sugar addiction, the ability to follow her counsel came solely through the sustaining power of the Lord. Without Him, this program would've been just one more failed diet. I know it was only through His strength that I broke free from the addictive chains that held me bound.[7]

It's hard to put into words exactly what this incredible, Christ-given freedom feels like. I think the best way to capture it is in the small moments, like when I pass up a plate of warm, gooey chocolate chip cookies, not because I'm relying on white-knuckle willpower, but because they just don't look that appetizing anymore. Moments like that still amaze me. After all, I'm the girl who couldn't *ever* say no to chocolate. I'm the girl with absolutely no self-control. I'm the girl who was convinced I'd take my food issues with me to the grave. But now, through the Lord's life-changing power, I'm a new person, a different person, one who's been freed from an appetite I could never conquer on my own. Like our little analogy about the king's banquet, I'm no longer trying to stuff my soul hunger with Twinkies and M&M's, and it's freed me to partake of the feast of Christ, which is a banquet unlike anything I've ever imagined.

The truth that finally penetrated my thick skull is that self-control isn't a matter of willpower. Instead, it's a *"fruit of the Spirit"* (see Galatians 5:22–23, footnote 23b). In other words, self-control can only come *from God.* All my life I'd set goals and made myself promises and got myself all psyched up to give up sweets, only to fail over and over and over again. Once I realized that rather than mustering up self-control on my own, I could receive it as a gift of the Spirit, things dramatically changed. Through the grace of the Lord, I've now been free from my sugar addiction for almost ten years. To me, that statement is more miraculous than the parting of the Red Sea. It just goes to show that Christ really is the only one who can help us overcome the persistent and insatiable appetites of our stubborn natural man.

With that said, I'll confess that the healing of my sugar addiction wasn't the only benefit I received as I filled myself at the Lord's banquet table. Though it was definitely the biggest hurdle I needed to tackle in dealing with my messed-up diet, I soon discovered that my Redeemer was only getting started in overhauling the way I looked at food. The Spirit's next instruction was simple yet shocking. In essence, I was told to *never go on a diet ever again.*

As stunned as I was to receive such a prompting, it dawned on me that dieting is the world's idea, not the Lord's. There's not one "thou shalt diet to lose weight" verse in all of scripture. Since I'd already learned for myself that diets don't work, I was thrilled to turn my back on this useless, discouraging practice.

What the Spirit helped me understand was that my body would respond best not to me starving it but to eating *the right kind of food*. I'm talking about the nourishment highlighted in the Word of Wisdom, including "every herb in the season thereof, and every fruit in the season thereof," and grain, which is "the staff of life . . . for man" (D&C 89:11, 14). Through the pages of the Doctrine and Covenants, the Lord had already laid out the perfect plan of health, but I'd ignored it in favor of counting calories and carbs and fat grams. At last, I realized it was time for me to quit listening to the world's views on health and study the simple truths laid out in the Word of Wisdom. Let me share with you a few of the things that I learned.

Did you know that back in 1938, Elder John A. Widtsoe wrote a book on the Word of Wisdom with his wife, Leah? In its pages, one of the Apostle's main concerns was the use of refined and processed food:

> Too much of the modern food supply comes from tin cans or packages, for often women as well as men work in factories and offices, and the can opener is coming to be the most used kitchen implement. Certain classes of our so-called civilized people . . . have come to subsist in large measure upon a diet of soft, highly refined and concentrated foods, a diet which is often predominantly acid-forming, lacking in fiber or residue and poor in mineral salts and vitamins. A typical modern diet of meat, white bread, refined cereals, potatoes and sweets, crowding milk, fruits and vegetables to a minimum, is especially likely to be deficient in calcium (and other minerals), roughage and vitamins. The results are unquestionably bad.[8]

As I read his words, I thought about how we hear a lot today about avoiding the dreaded fat in our diets, but we don't hear as much about refined or processed food. I'd like to suggest that's where the greatest threat to our health actually lies. Let me qualify that assertion with the words of bestselling author Michael Pollan in his book, *In Defense of Food: An Eater's Manifesto.* Pollan writes:

> In the midst of our deepening confusion about nutrition, it might be useful to step back and gaze upon it—review what we *do* know about the Western diet and its effects on our health. What we know is that people who eat the way we do in the West today suffer substantially higher rates of cancer, cardiovascular diseases, diabetes, and obesity than people eating any number of different traditional diets. We also know that when people come to the West and adopt our way of eating, these diseases soon follow, and often . . . in a particularly virulent form. . . .
>
> Some [researchers] noted that the Western diseases followed closely on the heels of the arrival of Western foods, particularly refined flour and sugar and other kinds of "store food." They observed too that when one Western disease arrived on the scene, so did most of the others, and often in the same order: obesity followed by type 2 diabetes followed by hypertension and stroke followed by heart disease.[9]

Pollan proves his point by highlighting the work of Dr. Weston A. Price, a dentist who became convinced that the Western diet was responsible for the rapid increase in dental problems that arrived around the turn of the century. To investigate this theory, Price abandoned his dental practice and traveled the world in search of populations who'd never ingested white flour, refined sugar, or any other type of processed food. It was a journey that took him to Switzerland, Africa, Australia, New Zealand, Melanesia, Alaska, and everywhere in between. Pollan summarizes the doctor's findings this way:

> So what did Price learn? First, that isolated populations eating a wide variety of traditional diets had no need of dentists whatsoever. . . .
>
> Wherever he found an isolated primitive race that had not yet encountered the "displacing foods of modern commerce"—by which he meant refined flour, sugar, canned and chemically preserved foods, and vegetable oils—he found little or no evidence of "modern degeneration"—by which he meant chronic disease, tooth decay, and malformed dental arches.[10]

Imagine that. Whenever Price found a people that ate only unprocessed food, not only did he find no sign of tooth decay, he also found no sign of heart disease, diabetes, cancer, hypertension, or stroke. Price's research powerfully illustrates that our bodies were created to live on *real* food, not the refined and sugar-laden products that masquerade as nourishment in stores today.

My studies also led me to another problem with the Western diet, one that often goes unnoticed by even the most conscientious consumer. Elder Widstoe addressed this problem by spending an entire chapter on the "evils and designs which do and will exist in the hearts of conspiring men in the last days" (D&C 89:4). Here's one part of his persuasive argument:

> Modern knowledge has given man the power to refine his foods, until some of them may become very changed from the natural conditions in which they are found. The common use of such refined, and in most cases concentrated foods, has at times, for want of adequate knowledge, led to injurious results. Occasionally, also, unscrupulous advertising, unmindful of the facts in the case, has increased the possible danger from the unwise use of refined, concentrated food products. . . .
>
> The American nation is fast becoming a people who eat out of packages and cans and drink out of bottles, thus furnishing the opportunity for unscrupulous persons to practice fraud upon their fellowmen.
>
> The principles of the Word of Wisdom point securely to the safe and sane way to health through proper nutrition and the use of natural food products, without becoming subject to the attacks of frauds.[11]

Could it be that the "conspiring men" mentioned in the Word of Wisdom aren't just the tobacco companies and the alcohol manufacturers like we Mormons tend to think? Could it also include those who load the American diet with hidden sugars, preservatives, and flavor enhancers in an attempt to get us hooked on their nutritionally useless products? Perhaps it's time for us to take a look at the big picture with regard to our diets. In the words of President Ezra Taft Benson,

> To a great extent we are physically what we eat. Most of us are acquainted with some of the prohibitions [of the Word of Wisdom] such as no tea, coffee, tobacco, or alcohol. What needs additional emphasis are the positive aspects—the need for vegetables, fruits,

and grains, particularly wheat. In most cases, the closer these can be, when eaten, to their natural state—without overrefinement and processing—the healthier we will be. To a significant degree, we are an overfed and undernourished nation digging an early grave with our teeth, and lacking the energy that could be ours because we indulge in junk foods. . . . We need a generation . . . who, as Daniel, eat in a more healthy manner than to fare on the "king's meat"—and whose countenances show it.[12]

I can now stand as a witness of these truths. As I partook of the feast of the Lord by following the Word of Wisdom to the best of my understanding, I experienced some very dramatic changes in my physical body. As I continued to rely on the Lord to help me eat His way, I was surprised to find that my weight stabilized without any dieting whatsoever. In addition, my energy level shot through the roof, I began sleeping better at night, and I didn't get sick as much as I used to. I found that I enjoyed rediscovering the taste of real food, like the burst of sweetness in a ripe strawberry or the soothing comfort of a slice of whole wheat bread. It felt good to view food not as something to lust after but as something to fuel my body and keep it strong. Truly, the physical benefits I gained by following the Spirit's guidance have been nothing short of astounding.

However, as incredible as these physical changes have been, what's shocked me the most are all the *emotional* and *spiritual* changes that have come as a result of changing my diet. For one thing, I was stunned to watch my irritability and mood swings completely melt away, along with the month-long PMS and depression I'd battled for years. In its place, I discovered a mental clarity and a brightness of soul unlike anything I'd ever experienced. I also enjoy a heightened sensitivity to the Spirit and a vitality and enthusiasm far beyond my usual capacity. Put simply, I now feel lighter, happier, and more connected to the Lord. No longer do I need the high I used to get from chocolate. The feast of Christ—the vitality and abundance and joy and health I'm now experiencing through His abundant grace—is ten thousand times better. Through my Savior's power, I've truly been healed both body and soul.

Now, I know how women's brains work, which means some are reading this and thinking, "Hey, wait a minute. You haven't told me how many servings of vegetables you eat or what foods you use to jumpstart your metabolism. I need rules to follow. I need help to get me started on the right path." The reason I'm not giving specific details about my diet is because, when it comes to nutrition, what we need most is not another bandwagon to jump on but the personal revelation that will fit our own unique and individual needs.

You see, even though Dr. DesMaisons's plan was right for me, I recognize that not everyone has the same issues with sugar. So our ultimate goal is to stop heeding all the voices shouting at us to eat *this* way or *that* way, and to turn to the Lord for the truth we need most. Yes, He'll definitely base that revelation on the Word of Wisdom, but that section doesn't provide many specifics, so we need His help to know how to fit that information into our everyday lives. As you pray for guidance, perhaps the Spirit will direct you to a book or a class or a friend who has the information that will suit your personal needs. Or maybe He'll work with you one-on-one through the thoughts of your mind and the feelings of your heart. No matter what avenue He uses, there's one truth that will never vary for each of us: in order to partake of the feast of Christ, we must fast from the lusts of our flesh and turn to the Lord. Nourishing ourselves physically by eating in accordance with the Word of Wisdom is an important aspect of that feast. As we follow the Word of Wisdom the Lord will keep His promise to give us "health in [the] navel and marrow to [the] bones," He'll pour out "wisdom and great treasures of knowledge, even hidden treasures," and we "shall run and not be weary, and shall walk and not faint" (D&C 89:19–20). In other words, if we'll turn our lives, and our diets, over to Christ, we'll be different; we'll be radiant; we'll be filled to overflowing with the beauty of the Lord.

One of the most important things I learned is that there's a sacred middle ground that exists between the extremes of body obsession and body neglect. It's a place of peace, a place of balance, and a place of incredible freedom. It's not the place I lived for most of my life. Instead, I spent all my time swinging from one extreme to the other. It felt like a pendulum: obsess, neglect, obsess, neglect, obsess, neglect. For instance, I'd pour everything I had into losing weight, then I'd break down and binge. I'd become fixated on a new workout plan, then I'd quit exercising altogether. I'd dress in hopes others would admire me, then I'd decide I looked terrible in every item of clothing I owned. No matter how hard I tried to avoid it, the pendulum just continued to swing back and forth.

But once the Lord took me under His wing and showed me how to care for my physical body, I discovered this wonderful middle ground beckoning me to come settle in. As tempting as it was to take the Spirit's nutritional guidance and turn it into my new obsession, I knew it was time to bring the pendulum to a stop once and for all. And the place it finally stopped for me was back at a size twelve. It's the size my body was meant to be—the shape that's right for me based on my lifestyle, my metabolism, and my genetics. Yes, I could probably be smaller, but only if I thought about food and exercise every minute of the day. And I now know that the Lord doesn't want me to live that way. With my mind caught up in counting calories and fat grams, and obsessing over my body size, I'm useless to Him. The only way I can be free is to embrace the real me.

Once I did so, I learned that life in this middle ground is better than I ever imagined it could be. No longer do I have to weigh myself every day, or scrutinize everything I eat, or muster up the willpower to starve myself on yet another miserable diet. Through the strength of my Savior, I eat real food when I'm hungry and I stop when I'm full (another thing I needed help with). I add in some exercise as often as possible, then I go about my day, completely free from all thoughts of food and dieting. Best of all, this freedom allows me to devote my mind and energy to the Lord rather than obsessing over a regulated food plan or an intense workout routine. I can hardly describe how exhilarating it is to have that heavy burden lifted off my shoulders. The pendulum has finally stopped swinging.[13]

Now, I'll admit that every once in a while, the adversary tries to tempt me to drift back to one extreme or the other. When that happens, I fight the temptation to obsess by recommitting to abstain from the lusts of my flesh, and I fend off body neglect by praying for strength to follow the health practices I've learned through the Spirit. The motivation to do so comes from knowing that only between these two extremes do I experience lasting peace; only between these extremes do I retain a liberating acceptance of my body; only between these extremes do I truly become a "temple of the living God" (2 Corinthians 6:16).

For Additional Study

Here's Sister Tanner's take on the two extremes we just discussed:

> [Satan's] punishment is that he does not have [a body]. Therefore he tries to do everything he can to get us to abuse or misuse this precious gift. He has filled the world with lies and deceptions about the body. He tempts many to defile this great gift of the body through unchastity, immodesty, self-indulgence, and addictions. He seduces some to despise their bodies; others he tempts to worship their bodies. In either case, he entices the world to regard the body merely as an object. In the face of so many satanic falsehoods about the body, I want to raise my voice today in support of the sanctity of the body. I testify that the body is a gift to be treated with gratitude and respect. . . .
>
> The pleasures of the body can become an obsession for some; so too can the attention we give to our outward appearance. Sometimes there is a selfish excess of exercising, dieting, makeovers, and spending money on the latest fashions (see Alma 1:27).
>
> I am troubled by the practice of extreme makeovers. Happiness comes from accepting the bodies we have been given as divine gifts and enhancing our natural attributes, not from remaking our bodies after the image of the world. The Lord wants us to be made over—but in His image, not in the image of the world, by receiving His image in our countenances. (see Alma 5:14, 19)[14]

Look up Ecclesiastes 10:18. Though this scripture is speaking of a building, how could it relate to the way you care for your physical body?

Next, read the following quotes, first from Elder David A. Bednar, then Elder L. Tom Perry. Consider how they tie in with the verse you just read in Ecclesiastes.

We are called to be, as the Apostle Peter wrote, "a royal priesthood, an holy nation, a peculiar people" (1 Peter 2:9). To be sure, we should be peculiar in the sense that we are distinctive, set apart from, and uncontrolled by the world. In addition, we are peculiar in a more powerful sense. As the Greek word implies, we are peculiar in that we are a purchased people.

Interestingly, I have heard many people, both outside and inside the Church, declare, 'It's my body and I can do to it what I want.' The correct doctrinal response to such a statement is quite simple. No, your body is not your own; it is on loan from God.[15]

Go and stand in front of a temple. Study carefully the house of the Lord and see if it does not inspire you to make some improvements in the physical temple the Lord has given to you to house your eternal spirit. The Lord has established some basic standards for the governance of our physical bodies. Obedience to these standards remains as a requirement for ordination to the priesthood, for a temple recommend, and for holding a calling in the Church.[16]

Now turn to Doctrine and Covenants 89. What do you learn in verse 3 about the Word of Wisdom? Have you ever felt too weak to eat the way you know you should? Where does that weakness come from? What can we do when we're feeling weak and discouraged? (See Ether 12:27 and 2 Corinthians 12:7–10 for some initial answers.)

I must admit that I always thought Doctrine and Covenants 89 was the only place that talked about food in the Standard Works, but I was wrong. Here are some additional verses that teach us about the diet God designed to keep mankind healthy and strong: Genesis 1:29, 9:2–3; Deuteronomy 12:15; 1 Timothy 4:3; Enos 1:21; Mosiah 10:4, 21:16; Helaman 6:12; Ether 9:17–18; Doctrine and Covenants 42:43; Doctrine and Covenants 49:18–21; and Moses 2:29.

Take a minute to study Romans 14:17; 1 Corinthians 10:31; and Philippians 3:19. In what ways could Paul's counsel affect not only the way you eat but how you look at food in general? Now turn to Matthew 6:25 and evaluate how the Savior's words could apply to the way you manage your diet.

Before we conclude this discussion, let me point out one way the temple doesn't align itself with the way we care for our body. The temple grounds are always perfectly groomed without a weed in sight. If we take this comparison too seriously, it could lead us right back to body obsession where we think we need to look perfect every minute of every day. But mortality just doesn't work that way. Sometimes we need to work hard and get dirty. Sometimes we won't make it to the shower because we're busy caring for a house full of sick kids. Sometimes we need to leave our makeup on the counter and focus on more pressing matters. Remember, our goal is to live *between* the two extremes in a land of moderation, not obsessive perfection.

Finally, I want to include the link to an article that greatly influenced the way I view dieting and nutrition. Christian author Leslie Ludy draws the perfect balance between the extremes of physical neglect and body obsession. I simply want to shout a huge "Amen!" to everything she has to say: http://setapartgirl.com/ magazine/article/01-1-12/time-wasters-part-eight.

If your battle with food still seems impossible to overcome, I'd highly recommend the Church's 12 Step Addiction Recovery Program. Don't be scared away by the name of this program and assume that it's only for those who struggle with pornography or alcoholism. It's actually designed for anyone who needs to break the chains of an addictive substance, behavior, or habit. I've been working with our local Eating Support group for a while now, and I have to say that I love seeing hope spring into the eyes in those who have felt hopeless and trapped by the bondage of food. The support of other members of the group is incredibly comforting and encouraging. Try it. I know this Christ-centered program is powerful enough to help you overcome your personal struggles with food, whatever they may be.[17]

Filled with Light

As I write these words, it's summertime in Idaho. On most summer mornings, you'll find me soaking up some quiet time in my front room where I can enjoy the sunrise. My favorite days are those when the sky is filled with pinks and oranges and reds. It truly takes my breath away. For a few short moments, my soul drinks in the exquisite beauty and creativity of a loving God. It seems like my Father painted the sky simply to bring a smile to my face. It always does.

In fact, this morning the light was so intense, its beams seemed to penetrate straight into my heart. And it got me thinking about the power of light. So I did what most people do when they're curious about something: I looked it up on Wikipedia. Although I couldn't understand much of the scientific jargon I found there, I grinned when I learned that, in physics, light is called "radiant energy."[1] Wouldn't you agree that's something we all could use a little more of in our everyday lives?

Keeping with the theme of light, let me take you back to Isaiah chapter 58, that wonderful chapter on fasting and its subsequent blessings. I want to show you one of the blessings I never noticed until today. Maybe it was the sunrise, but this morning I found something hidden in those verses that immediately started turning the wheels of my mind. If you remember, Isaiah speaks of broken yokes, lifted burdens, restored health, answered prayers, satisfied souls, and even bones being made fat (Isaiah 58:9–11). But the part I missed, until today, was the part about *light*. Notice the promises: "then shall *thy light* break forth as the morning, . . . then shall *thy light* rise in obscurity, and thy darkness be as the noonday" (verses 8, 10). Thy light. *My* light. What, exactly, is Isaiah talking about? How does my light break forth like the sunrise I watched this morning? If we'll turn to the scriptures, we'll find they contain a really incredible answer.

Throughout the Standard Works, light is most often tied to the Lord Jesus Christ, since He is "the true light, which lighteth every man that cometh into the world" (John 1:9). As President Henry B. Eyring taught,

> Every child of Heavenly Father born in the world is given at birth, as a free gift, the Light of Christ. You have felt that. It is the sense of what is right and what is wrong and what is true and what is false. That has been with you since your journey in life began.[2]

Many other scriptures speak of Christ's ability to fill us with light. The Psalmist tells us, "For thou wilt light my candle: the Lord my God will enlighten my darkness" (Psalm 18:28). Isaiah encourages us, "Arise, shine; for thy light is come, and the glory of the Lord is risen upon thee" (Isaiah 60:1). And another of my favorite verses about light comes from the book of Job:

> He will deliver his soul from going into the pit, and his life shall see light.
> Lo, all these things worketh God oftentimes with man,
> To bring back his soul from the pit, to be enlightened with the light of the living. (Job 33:28–30)

The imagery of this passage is powerful. I think we've all had days where we longed to be brought out of the pit and "enlightened with the light of the living." What if I told you there's much more to this "enlightening" than you might think? What if I told you that Christ can fill our bodies so full of light, we'll never feel a sense of darkness or heaviness ever again? If that sounds a little over the top, you don't have to take my word for it. Here's the actual promise from the Lord Himself: "And if your eye be single to my glory, *your whole bodies shall be filled with light*, and *there shall be no darkness in you*" (D&C 88:67; italics added). If you ask me, that's a pretty mind-blowing possibility.

Just picture what it would feel like to have your whole body saturated with heavenly light. A good way to visualize it would be to stay with our temple theme and think about your favorite temple when it's lit up at night. It's quite a sight to behold, isn't it? Nothing stirs my heart like the radiant glow of our temple shining from the crest of the Rexburg hill. Can you imagine having your whole body illuminated like that? Can you imagine the intense joy you'd experience? It seems almost too good to be true. But it's not.

Time and time again, the scriptures reveal followers of Christ who have experienced this deep and lasting infusion of light. First, consider the people of Alma: "Behold, he changed their hearts; yea, he awakened them out of a deep sleep, and they awoke unto God. Behold, they were in the midst of darkness; nevertheless, *their souls were illuminated by the light of the everlasting word*" (Alma 5:7).

Then there's the Anti-Nephi-Lehies we spoke of earlier, the ones who faithfully buried their swords:

> And ye know also that they have buried their weapons of war, and they fear to take them up lest by any means they should sin; yea, ye can see that they fear to sin—for behold they will suffer themselves that they be trodden down and slain by their enemies, and will not lift their swords against them, and this because of their faith in Christ.
>
> And now, because of their steadfastness when they do believe in that thing which they do believe, for because of their firmness *when they are once enlightened,* behold, the Lord shall bless them and prolong their days. (Helaman 15:9–10)

In these verses, the people are described as being "illuminated" and "enlightened." Both words carry the meaning of being filled to overflowing with light. To help you picture what this feels like, I looked up some synonyms for the word *enlighten.* They include *enliven, brighten*, and *irradiate*.[3] In other words, the people were lit up both body and spirit. Like the definition of light I mentioned earlier, those who've been illuminated have the "radiant energy" of Christ shining in their souls. Their body is filled with the light the Lord teaches about in the Doctrine and Covenants. It's important to remember that the light we're talking about here is no small thing. The scriptures explain it this way:

> This is the light of Christ. As also he is in the sun, and the light of the sun, and the power thereof by which it was made.
>
> As also he is in the moon, and is the light of the moon, and the power thereof by which it was made;
>
> As also the light of the stars, and the power thereof by which they were made;
>
> And the earth also, and the power thereof, even the earth upon which you stand.
>
> And the light which shineth, which giveth you light, is through him who enlighteneth your eyes, which is the same light that quickeneth your understandings;
>
> Which light proceedeth forth from the presence of God to fill the immensity of space—
>
> The light which is in all things, which giveth life to all things, which is the law by which all things are governed, even the power of God who sitteth upon his throne, who is in the bosom of eternity, who is in the midst of all things. (D&C 88:7–13)

Just imagine, your body can actually be filled with the light of the sun, an orb so intense that we struggle to look at it with our natural eyes. Talk about radiant energy. Do you understand what an unfathomable blessing we're being offered here? It's the very blessing Lamoni obtained in the pages of the Book of Mormon. Listen as Mormon captures the young king's life-changing experience:

> For [Ammon] knew that king Lamoni was under the power of God; he knew that the dark veil of unbelief was being cast away from his mind, and the light which did light up his mind, which was the light of the glory of God, which was a marvelous light of his goodness—yea, this light had infused such joy into his soul, the cloud of darkness having been dispelled, and that the light of everlasting life was lit up in his soul, yea, he knew that this had overcome his natural frame, and he was carried away in God. (Alma 19:6)

Such a description leaves us breathless with anticipation and makes us yearn to join Lamoni in tasting this soul-filling light for ourselves.

How do we obtain this infusion of light, you ask? We'll find the answer by returning to the Savior's words. He said, "*if your eye be single to my glory*, your whole bodies shall be filled with light."

But what does it mean to have an eye *single* to His glory? While we may think the phrase means being focused or centered on Christ, Elder James E. Talmage taught that it represents our being "pure and undimmed by sin."[4]

The transformation process we've been walking through has already started us moving in that direction. Believe it or not, by allowing the Lord to remove our false beliefs and replace them with truth, and by burying our swords and fasting from the propaganda of the image, what we've really been doing is *repenting*. Remember, the word *repent* "denotes a change of mind, i.e., a fresh view about God, about oneself, and about the world."[5] So because we've cleansed our bodies and souls from all traces of the image, and because we've experienced a "change of mind" about ourselves and our physical bodies, we're on our way to becoming one who is "pure and undimmed by sin." Soon we'll be prepared to experience the very feast of light that the Lord promised. It's an extraordinary blessing—a very powerful gift from the incomparable Savior of the world.

At this moment, we've reached the final step in understanding the beauty of the Lord, since nothing compares to a woman lit up with the transcendent light of Christ. It shines through her eyes and reaches into the hearts of everyone around her. No longer do others define her by her hair color or body shape. Instead they recognize her as a true woman of God; a woman who knows who she is in Christ; a woman conformed, not to the image of the world but "to the image of his Son" (Romans 8:29). That's because she's been "changed into [His] image from glory to glory, even as by the Spirit of the Lord" (2 Corinthians 3:18). Such beauty is breathtaking, mesmerizing. It's far beyond the shallow, fictitious beauty of the world.

In the end, the transformation process is about much more than accepting the size of our feet or the shape of our hips. It's about finding out who we really are. And that is something that can only be discovered through Jesus Christ. Only in Him can we find our real selves, our most beautiful selves. Only in Him can we see our physical bodies as they were truly meant to be.

Let's not forget that the Lord knows exactly what we're going through when it comes to our outward appearance. After all, Isaiah said, "he hath no form nor comeliness; and when we shall see him, there is no beauty that we should desire him" (Isaiah 53:2). While the Jews may not have been impressed by the way Jesus looked, I think we've learned by now that Christ's tabernacle of flesh reflected nothing of His true beauty and majesty and power. Instead, let's picture Him the way John did on the day when He finally appears in glory:

> And I saw heaven opened, and behold a white horse; and he that sat upon him was called Faithful and True, and in righteousness he doth judge and make war.
>
> His eyes were as a flame of fire, and on his head were many crowns; and he had a name written, that no man knew, but he himself.
>
> And he was clothed with a vesture dipped in blood: and his name is called The Word of God...
>
> And out of his mouth goeth a sharp sword, that with it he should smite the nations: and he shall rule them with a rod of iron: and he treadeth the winepress of the fierceness and wrath of Almighty God.
>
> And he hath on his vesture and on his thigh a name written, King of Kings, and Lord of Lords. (Revelation 19:11–13, 15–16)

We must remember that we worship the astonishing, light-bearing, power-filled, awe-inspiring King of kings. And this King wants nothing more than to cleanse us from the shame, guilt, and shallowness of the worldly image. He longs to teach us of our true beauty *in Him*, to fill us both body and soul with His enduring, life-giving light. I've experienced this illumination for myself, and I have to say that there's nothing in the world that can make a woman feel more beautiful than having the light of her King infused into the depths of her soul. So I say with David, "the king greatly desire[s] thy beauty: for he is thy Lord; . . . *worship thou him*" (Psalm 45:11; italics added).

For Additional Study

With regard to light, Elder Robert D. Hales observed:

> The Lord is our light and, literally, our salvation. Like the sacred fire that encircled the children in 3 Nephi, His light will form a

protective shield between you and the darkness of the adversary as you live worthy of it. You need that light. We need that light.[6]

Add to that these wonderful words from President James E. Faust:

Alma asks if we have received His image in our countenances. A sacred light comes to our eyes and countenances when we have a personal bond with our loving Heavenly Father and His Son, our Savior and Redeemer. With this bond our faces will mirror that "sublime assurance" that He lives.[7]

Finally, consider this insight from the Doctrine and Covenants:

That which is of God is light; and he that receiveth light, and continueth in God, receiveth more light; and that light groweth brighter and brighter until the perfect day. (D&C 50:23–24)

How much of the Lord's light do you think you've already received? Do you believe you've reached the pinnacle of this heavenly light, or could there be much more waiting to be experienced? Is there anything holding you back from having your inner light grow "brighter and brighter"?

A Plea for the Next Generation

I speak now not only to mothers of daughters but to those who will someday raise a daughter, to those who will serve in Young Women or at Girls Camp, and to those who will interact in any way with the rising generation. You must know, whether you like it or not, you are being watched. You can't avoid it. The words you speak about yourself, the way you dress, the food you eat, and your opinion of physical beauty all have a profound and lasting impact on the impressionable girls growing up in your midst. The question is: Are you prepared for this responsibility that's been laid on your shoulders?

I heard a story once by the late actress and comedienne Gilda Radner that's remained with me ever since. Her message has a great deal to say with regard to the influence we leaders and mothers will have on the next generation:

> When I was little, Dibby's cousin had a dog, just a mutt, and the dog was pregnant. I don't know how long dogs are pregnant, but she was due to have her puppies in about a week. She was out in the yard one day and got in the way of the lawn mower, and her two hind legs got cut off. They rushed her to the vet and he said, "I can sew her up, or you can put her to sleep if you want, but the puppies are okay. She'll be able to deliver the puppies."
>
> Dibby's cousin said, "Keep her alive."
>
> So the vet sewed up her backside and over the next week the dog learned to walk. She didn't spend any time worrying, she just

learned to walk by taking two steps in the front and flipping up her backside, and then taking two steps and flipping up her backside again. She gave birth to six little puppies, all in perfect health. She nursed them and then weaned them. And when they learned to walk, *they all walked like her.*[1]

Every one of us must face the stark reality that our daughters are being bombarded by the message of the image. And they will learn how to respond to that message by watching *us.* We can't teach them one thing and do another. We can't cross our fingers and hope that they won't inherit our body insecurities or our issues with food. If we buy into the world's standard of beauty, so will they. If we talk about how fat we are, so will they. If we mistreat or devalue or criticize our physical body, so will they. In the words of Elder Jeffrey R. Holland, "if you are obsessing over being a size 2, you won't be very surprised when your daughter or the Mia Maid in your class does the same and makes herself physically ill trying to accomplish it."[2] It's a dynamic that we women can't escape, no matter how much we may want to.

In the April 2010 general conference, Elder M. Russell Ballard said this about the power of a mother's influence:

Young women behave like their mothers. If the mothers are thrifty, so are their daughters. If the mothers are modest, so are the girls. If the mothers wear flip-flops and other casual clothing to sacrament meeting, so do their daughters. Mothers, your example is extremely important to your daughters—even if they don't acknowledge it.[3]

He then continued by giving this important direction:

Throughout the history of the world, women have always been teachers of moral values. That instruction begins in the cradle and continues throughout the lives of their children. Today our society is bombarded with messages about womanhood and motherhood that are dangerously and wickedly wrong. Following these messages can put your daughters on the path to sin and self-destruction. Your daughters may not understand that unless you tell them or, better, *unless you show them* how to make good choices. As mothers in Israel, you are your daughters' first line of defense against the wiles of the world.[4]

Notice that we can't just tell them. We have to *show* them. And we show them first and foremost by breaking free from the chains of the image ourselves. It's like the flight attendant tells the passengers before takeoff: if a need for the oxygen masks arises, first put on your own mask, and *then* assist your children. The only way we can help the next generation is to first find healing and freedom in our own individual hearts and minds.

Elder Ballard also said something in his talk that was directed to young women. His counsel should give us pause as we consider the message he's sending to mothers as well:

> My dear young women, with all my heart I urge you not to look to contemporary culture for your role models and mentors. Please look to your faithful mothers for a pattern to follow. Model yourselves after them, not after celebrities whose standards are not the Lord's standards and whose values may not reflect an eternal perspective. Look to your mother. Learn from her strengths, her courage, and her faithfulness. Listen to her. . . . No other person on earth loves you in the same way or is willing to sacrifice as much to encourage you and help you find happiness—in this life and forever.[5]

Do the Apostle's words leave you trembling just a little? As difficult as it may be to hear, I must ask, what kind of example are you when it comes to modeling the beauty of the Lord? Do you have something to say that will counteract the voices of the world? Or are you too busy buying into those voices yourself? Sisters, I ask with all the love in my heart, if we continually deride our looks and put down our appearance, how will our daughters learn to believe they're beautiful just the way they are? If we cope with stress by using food, how will our daughters learn to handle adversity by turning to Christ? If we're not at peace with the effects of childbearing or aging, how will our daughters learn to navigate that difficult territory themselves? If we count every calorie and fat gram we put in our mouths, how will our daughters learn that the purpose of food is to gladden the heart and enliven the soul? If we heed the messages society sends us about our bodies, how will our daughters learn to tune out the persistent voices of the world?

Like it or not, *we* are the role models of beauty in Christ. If we don't illustrate it, no one will. If we haven't yet found the courage to start our own personal path to healing, maybe we'll find it now for our daughters' sake. Then, in contrast to the dog in Ms. Radner's story, we can actually teach our vulnerable puppies to walk the right way.

I often wonder why we aren't getting angrier about what Satan is doing to the sensitive hearts and minds of women. I'd like to suggest that there's nothing wrong with allowing a little righteous indignation to fill us and equip us for the battle. The problem, according to the Doctrine and Covenants, is this:

> Behold, I have commanded my servant Joseph Smith, Jun., to say unto the strength of my house, even my warriors, . . . to gather together for the redemption of my people, and throw down the towers of mine enemies, and scatter their watchmen;
> *But the strength of mine house have not hearkened unto my words.*
> (D&C 105:16–17; italics added)

Perhaps it's time to draw our swords for battle. Perhaps it's time to stand on our feet and say, "No more!" As women, we know we possess a fierceness when it comes to protecting our children. Maybe it's time to let the mother tiger in us bare her claws. Remember, Satan is coming for our daughters, not just us. He wants to infiltrate their minds and fill their hearts with shame. And if you look at the statistics surrounding teenage anorexia, bulimia, chronic dieting, and negative body image, I'd say he's already imprisoned far too many young women. Well, I say it's time to fight back. Time to arm ourselves with "righteousness and with the power of God in great glory" (1 Nephi 14:14). Time to win back a few of those prisoners, especially if we've been numbered among those captives ourselves.

However, the only way we'll be able to do this is through the power of Jesus Christ. We've watched ourselves fail on our own. We've watched ourselves spin our wheels, muster up more willpower, and still remain chained, insecure, and miserable. No, for this particular battle, we need *supernatural* power. We need One who can cast out demons, heal the lame, and walk on water. We need the insight, strength, and life-changing truth *of Christ*. In fact, we don't just need Him to walk by our sides—we need to truly "abide in [Him], and [He] in [us]" (John 15:4).

Mothers, leaders, and mentors of young women, our goal is simple: we must come to Christ and let Him teach us how to treat our bodies as temples (D&C 93:35). We must come to Christ and let Him silence the negative voices in our heads (Philippians 4:7). We must come to Christ and learn how to rejoice in our God-given femininity (Proverbs 31:10–31). We must come to Christ and discover an acceptance of our personal sizes and shapes (Isaiah 26:3). We must come to Christ and let Him still our minds and calm our emotions so we no longer need to turn to food or any other crutches (Ephesians 4:22–24). We must come to Christ and let Him support us through the physical changes of pregnancy, illness, and aging (Psalms 103:14). We must come to Christ and hear how our bodies are fearfully and wonderfully made (Psalms 139:14). Most of all, we must come to Christ and finally know for ourselves what it's like to be draped in the transcendent beauty of the Lord.

We do this by carving out the time needed to let Christ's healing balm seep into the farthest reaches of our battle-weary hearts. We do it by asking for His help to shatter all our false beliefs, to recognize and confess our sins, and to rely day by day on His glorious and empowering grace. We do it by choosing to fast from all the propaganda of the image, and by giving up our metaphorical Twinkies in favor of His soul-filling banquet. Though the process may look different for each of us, if we'll turn to Christ and "present [our] bodies a living sacrifice," we'll no longer "be . . . conformed to this world," but we'll be "transformed by the renewing of [our] mind[s]" (Romans 12:1). I promise that once we partake of this incredible feast, we—along with our daughters—will never be the same ever again.

Additional Reading

I've provided the following list of references because these books introduced me to a whole new way of seeing things like dieting, nutrition, hormones, sickness, disease, and medicine. These authors share information that is almost never discussed in the mainstream media, and I believe it's information we desperately need to have. (I promise you'll never see a box of cold cereal or a can of soda the same way again!)

However, by recommending these publications, that doesn't mean I endorse every point the authors make or I've adopted every proposal they suggest. Instead, I believe we should approach these types of works the same way the Lord taught us to handle the Apocrypha:

> Verily, thus saith the Lord unto you concerning the Apocrypha— There are many things contained therein that are true, and it is mostly translated correctly; . . . Therefore, whoso readeth it, let him understand, for the Spirit manifesteth truth; And whoso is enlightened by the Spirit shall obtain benefit therefrom. (D&C 91:1–2, 4–6)

So, if you feel prompted to read any of the works cited here, I beg you to do so with the Spirit as your guide. This is crucial because many of the authors write in a dogmatic and uncompromising way, which can make the reader feel overwhelmed or discouraged by the things that they're reading. At least, that's what happened to me. Thankfully, as I continued to rely on the Lord, He showed me how to make small changes that both my family and our finances could handle without becoming overwhelmed. I know that if you'll stay close to the Lord, He'll direct you to the information that fits your individual needs, and He'll also provide the wisdom, strength, and discipline to follow the guidance you receive.

References

Many of these books can be found in your local library. Also, each one has a Kindle edition on amazon.com.

Gary Taubes, *Good Calories, Bad Calories: Challenging the Conventional Wisdom on Diet, Weight Control, and Disease* (New York, NY: Alfred A. Knopf, 2007). I believe this is one of the most important books you could ever read on the subject of health and nutrition. For a more condensed version, try Taubes's book *Why We Get Fat: And What To Do About It* (New York, NY: Anchor Books, 2011).

Robert H. Lustig, *Fat Chance: Beating the Odds Against Sugar, Processed Food, Obesity, and Disease* (New York, NY: Hudson Street Press, 2013).

Michael Moss, *Sugar Salt Fat: How the Food Giants Hooked Us* (New York, NY: Random House, 2013).

Melanie Warner, *Pandora's Lunchbox: How Processed Food Took over the American Meal* (New York, NY: Scribner, 2013).

Kathleen DesMaisons, *The Sugar Addict's Total Recovery Program* (New York, NY: Ballantine Books, 2002). Dr. DesMaisons has actually written several books on this subject, including one designed especially for children. You can find more information on her website, radiantrecovery.com.

Connie Bennett, *Sugar Shock! How Sweets and Simple Carbs Can Derail Your Life—and How You Can Get Back on Track* [New York, NY: Berkley Books, 2007].

Jack Challem, *The Food-Mood Solution: All-Natural Ways to Banish Anxiety, Depression, Anger, Stress, Overeating, and Alcohol and Drug Problems—and Feel Good Again* (Hoboken, NJ: John Wiley & Sons, Inc., 2007).

Richard Shames and Karilee Shames, *Feeling Fat, Fuzzy, or Frazzled?: A 3-Step Program to: Restore Thyroid, Adrenal, and Reproductive Balance, Beat Hormone Havoc, and Feel Better Fast!* (New York, NY: Hudson Street Press, 2005).

Jonny Bowden and Stephen Sinatra, *The Great Cholesterol Myth: Why Lowering Your Cholesterol Won't Prevent Heart Disease—And the Statin-Free Plan That Will* (Beverly, MA: Fair Winds Press, 2012).

Dr. H. Gilbert Welch, Dr. Lisa M. Schwartz, and Dr. Steven Woloshin, *Overdiagnosed: Making People Sick in the Pursuit of Health* (Boston, MA: Beacon Press, 2011).

References

Ray Moynihan and Alan Cassels, *Selling Sickness: How the World's Biggest Pharmaceutical Companies Are Turning Us All Into Patients* (New York, NY: Nation Books, 2005).

Paul Campos, *The Obesity Myth: Why America's Obsession with Weight is Hazardous to Your Health* (New York, NY: Gotham Books, 2004).

Dr. John R. Lee, M.D. and Virginia Hopkins, *What Your Doctor May Not Tell You About Premenopause: Balance Your Hormones and your Life from Thirty to Fifty* (New York, NY: Time Warner Book Group, 2005). Dr. Lee has also written a version of this book for women who are going through menopause.

Michael Pollan, *In Defense of Food: An Eater's Manifesto* (New York, NY: Penguin Books, 2008). Pollan's books *The Omnivore's Dilemma* and *Food Rules: An Eater's Manual* are also very good.

Nina Planck, *Real Food: What to Eat and Why* (New York, NY: Bloomsbury, 2006).

Sally Fallon and Mary Enig, *Nourishing Traditions: The Cookbook that Challenges Politically Correct Nutrition and the Diet Dictocrats* (Washington, D.C.: Newtrends Publishing, 1999).

Catherine Shanahan and Luke Shanahan, *Deep Nutrition: Why Your Genes Need Traditional Food* (Lawai, HI: Big Box Books, 2009).

Catherine Shanahan, *Food Rules: A Doctor's Guide to Healthy Eating* (CreateSpace Independent Publishing Platform, 2010).

Gretchen Reynolds, *The First 20 Minutes: Surprising Science Reveals How We Can Exercise Better, Train Smarter, Live Longer* (New York, NY: Hudson Street Press, 2012). This book dispelled many of the myths I've always believed about physical exercise.

Ellen Barrett and Kate Hanley, *The 28 Days Lighter Diet: Your Monthly Plan to Lose Weight, End PMS, and Achieve Physical and Emotional Wellness* (Guilford, CT: Globe Pequot Press, 2014). Despite the title, this isn't really a diet book. It's an incredibly unique look at a woman's monthly cycle. The authors explain how women can eat and exercise in a way that honors their cycle rather than ignoring it or fighting against it. It's a very interesting read, although a bit PG-13 at times.

Endnotes

The Ghost in the Checkout Line

1 Jeffrey R. Holland, "To Young Women," *Ensign,* November 2005, 28–30.

2 Lisa Bevere, *You Are Not What You Weigh: End Your War with Food and Discover Your True Value* (Lake Mary, FL: Siloam, 1996), 28–29.

3 Nicole Hawkins, "Battling our Bodies: Understanding and Overcoming Negative Body Images," centerforchange.com, accessed July 1, 2013, http://www.centerforchange.com/news-resources/newsletter/battling-our-bodies-understanding-and-overcoming-negative-body-images.

4 "About Eating Disorders," The Eating Disorder Foundation, accessed November 21, 2013, http://www.eatingdisorderfoundation.org/EatingDisorders.htm. See also http://www.nationaleatingdisorders.org/get-facts-eating-disorders.

5 "Beauty Redefined: Rejecting the Media's Impossible Standards," Lexie Kite, PhD and Lindsay Kite, PhD, codirectors of the Beauty Redefined Foundation, *LDS Living Magazine*, accessed January 22, 2011, http://www.ldsliving.com/story/63275-beauty-redefined-rejecting-the-medias-impossible-standards.

Babylon in the 21st Century

1 "Photoshopping: Altering Images and Our Minds!," Lexie Kite, PhD and Lindsay Kite, PhD, codirectors of the Beauty Redefined Foundation, beautyredefined.net, accessed January 22, 2011, http://www.beautyredefined.net/photoshopping-altering-images-and-our-minds.

2 Amy Wallace, "Jamie Lee Curtis: True Thighs," *MORE Magazine*, accessed June 24, 2011, http://www.more.com/news/womens-issues/jamie-lee-curtis-true-thighs.

3 Ibid.

4 Paul Campos, *The Obesity Myth: Why America's Obsession with Weight is Hazardous to Your Health* (New York, NY: Gotham Books, 2004), xvi-xix.

5 Ibid., 12.

6 Ibid., 13.

Endnotes

7 Ibid., 20.

8 Ibid., 24.

9 Ibid., 39.

10 J. Eric Oliver, *Fat Politics: The Real Story behind America's Obesity Epidemic* (Oxford University Press, 2006) 242w, 5. By permission of Oxford University Press, USA. www.oup.com.

11 Ibid, 6. By permission of Oxford University Press, USA. www.oup.com.

12 Eric A. Finkelstein and Laurie Zuckerman, *The Fattening of America: How The Economy Makes Us Fat, If It Matters and What To Do About It* (Hoboken: NJ: John Wiley & Sons, 2008), 204. Used by permission.

13 "Worship," World English Dictionary, http://dictionary.reference.com/browse/worship.

Portrait of an Image Worshipper

1 Evelyn Tribole and Elyse Resch, *Intuitive Eating: A Revolutionary Program That Works* (New York, NY: St. Martin's Press, 2003), 54. From INTUITIVE EATING © by Evelyn Tribole. Reprinted by permission of St. Martin's Press. All rights reserved.

2 Ibid., 54.

3 Debra Waterhouse, *Outsmarting the Female Fat Cell* (New York, NY: Warner Books, 1993), 13–14, 24.

4 Tribole and Resch, *Intuitive Eating*, 16.

5 Ibid., 9. Author Gary Taubes makes the same argument in his incredibly well-researched book *Good Calories, Bad Calories: Challenging the Conventional Wisdom on Diet, Weight Control, and Disease* (New York, NY: Alfred A. Knopf, 2007).

6 Paul Campos, *The Obesity Myth*, 128.

7 Tribole and Resch, *Intuitive Eating*, 9–13.

8 Michelle May, *Eat What You Love, Love What You Eat: How to Break Your Eat-Repent-Repeat Cycle* (Austin, TX: Greenleaf Book Group Press, 2010), 1.

9 Patricia T. Holland, *A Quiet Heart* (Salt Lake City, UT: Bookcraft, 2000), 61–62.

10 David A. Bednar, "Things As They Really Are," *Ensign*, June 2010. See also David A. Bednar, *Increase in Learning: Spiritual Patterns for Obtaining Your Own Answers* (Salt Lake City, UT: Deseret Book, 2011), 196–97.

11 Ibid.

Turning Glory into Shame

1 Nicole Unice, "I Gave Up Makeup for Lent," accessed June 6, 2011, http://www.nicoleunice.com/daily-life-with-jesus/i-gave-up-makeup-for-lent/.

2 "Conceal," World English Dictionary, http://dictionary.reference.com/browse/conceal.

Dressing for the Eyes of Others

1 I was first introduced to these and other wonderful facets of beauty by John and Stasi Eldredge, *Captivating: Unveiling the Mystery of a Woman's Soul* (Nashville, TN: Thomas Nelson, 2005), 37–41. Used by permission. All rights reserved.

2 Michelle Graham, *Wanting To Be Her: Body Image Secrets Victoria Won't Tell You* (Downers Grove, IL: InterVarsity Press, 2005), 90–91; Italics added.

3 Ibid., 91.

4 James E. Strong, *Strongest Strong's Exhaustive Concordance of the Bible* (Grand Rapids, MI: Zondervan, 2001), 1583.

5 *Merriam-Webster's Collegiate Dictionary*, Tenth Edition (Springfield, MA: Merriam Webster, 2000), 1326.

6 James E. Strong, *Strongest Strong's Exhaustive Concordance of the Bible* (Grand Rapids, MI: Zondervan, 2001), 1556.

7 Taken from *Who Calls Me Beautiful?*, © 2004 by Regina Franklin. Used by permission of Discovery House Publishers, Grand Rapids, MI 49501. All rights reserved.

8 James E. Strong, *Strongest Strong's Exhaustive Concordance of the Bible* (Grand Rapids, MI: Zondervan, 2001), 1543.

9 Regina Franklin, *Who Calls Me Beautiful*, 15 (italics added).

10 Jeffrey R. Holland, "To Young Women," *Ensign*, November 2005, 28–30.

Time for a Transformation

1 "Addictive Nature of Chocolate among Women," *Medical News* TODAY, accessed August 5, 2011, http://www.medicalnewstoday.com/articles/27571.php.

2 Patricia T. Holland, *A Quiet Heart*, 110.

It's All In Our Heads

1 Virginia H. Pearce, *Through His Eyes: Rethinking What You Believe about Yourself* (Salt Lake City, UT: Deseret Book, 2011), 18.

Endnotes

2 Ibid., 27.

3 Ibid., 38.

4 Ibid., 48.

5 Taken from: LOVE TO EAT, HATE TO EAT. Copyright ©1999 by Elyse Fitzpatrick. Published by Harvest House Publishers, Eugene, Oregon 97402. www. harvesthousepublishers.com. Used by permission.

6 "Mad TV Bob Newhart Skit – Mo Collins – Stop it," YouTube video, 6:15, posted by "ashoun," August 15, 2007, http://www.youtube.com/watch?v=BYLMTvxOaeE.

7 "Vain," World English Dictionary, http://dictionary.reference.com/browse/vain.

8 *Merriam-Webster's Collegiate Dictionary*, Tenth Edition (Springfield, MA:Merriam Webster, 2000), 987–88.

9 Ibid., 297.

A Lesson from the Book of Psalms

1 James E. Strong, *Strongest Strong's Exhaustive Concordance of the Bible* (Grand Rapids, MI: Zondervan, 2001), 1516. See also Revelation 2:23, footnote b.

2 Taken from *LOVING YOUR BODY: EMBRACING YOUR TRUE BEAUTY IN CHRIST* by Dr. Deborah Newman. Copyright © 2002 by Dr. Deborah Newman. Used by permission of Tyndale House Publishers, Inc. All rights reserved.

3 James E. Strong, *Strongest Strong's Exhaustive Concordance of the Bible* (Grand Rapids, MI: Zondervan, 2001), 1630.

4 "Grace," LDS Church, Bible Dictionary, LDS Scriptures, 697.

5 Oswald Chambers, *My Utmost for His Highest* (Grand Rapids, MI: Discovery House, 1992), 2/27; italics added.

Burying Our Swords

1 *Merriam-Webster's Collegiate Dictionary*, Tenth Edition (Springfield, MA: Merriam Webster, 2000), 5.

2 One of the most insightful chapters I've ever read on food as a false god is by Kyle Idleman, "The God of Food," *Gods at War: Defeating the Idols That Battle for Your Heart* (Grand Rapids, MI: Zondervan, 2013).

3 James E. Strong, *Strongest Strong's Exhaustive Concordance of the Bible* (Grand Rapids, MI: Zondervan, 2001), 1611. See also W. E. Vine, *Vine's Complete Expository Dictionary of Old and New Testament Words* (Nashville, TN: Nelson, 1984), 384.

4 For more on this idea, see Romans 13:14; Galatians 5:24; and 1 John 2:16.

5 "Forsake," World English Dictionary, http://dictionary.reference.com/browse/forsake?s=t.

Beauty for Ashes

1 John and Stasi Eldredge, *Captivating: Unveiling the Mystery of a Woman's Soul* (Nashville, TN: Thomas Nelson, 2005), 132–133.

2 "Neat," World English Dictionary, http://dictionary.reference.com/browse/neat?s=t.

3 "Comely," World English Dictionary, http://dictionary.reference.com/browse/comely?s=t.

4 "Comely," World English Dictionary, http://thesaurus.com/browse/comely?s=t.

Between Two Extremes

1 "Temple Walk Challenge," *New Era*, July 2011, 26.

2 David A. Bednar, "Ye Are the Temple of God," *Ensign*, September 2001, 14–21.

3 Susan W. Tanner, "The Sanctity of the Body," *Ensign*, November 2005, 13.

4 Kathleen DesMaisons, *The Sugar Addict's Total Recovery Program* (New York, NY: Ballantine Books, 2000), 3–5.

5 John S. Tanner, "The Body as a Blessing," *Ensign*, July 1993, 10; quoted in Susan W. Tanner, "The Sanctity of the Body," *Ensign*, November 2005, 13; emphasis added.

6 For more evidence of the damage sugar does to our bodies, check out the books listed in the appendix. Several of the authors link sugar and refined carbohydrates to many of today's common ailments, including chronic killers like heart disease and cancer. And you don't just have to take their word for it, because they back up their claims with a huge collection of medical studies, articles, and expert opinion.

7 I believe another reason this program was successful for me is that the Spirit helped me adapt it to fit my individual needs. For instance, Dr. DesMaisons suggests you eat a potato every night to balance the serotonin in your brain—which definitely works—but I had a hard time with the thought of eating a potato every night for the rest of my life. So I've substituted other whole grain carbohydrates with great success. She also talks about journaling about what you eat, which helped a lot at first, but eventually I was prompted to give up this practice because it kept me way too focused on food. So if you're planning to try this program, I'd suggest you rely heavily on the Spirit's guidance. That way the Lord can help you adapt it to fit your own personal needs.

Endnotes

8 John A. and Leah D. Widstoe, *The Word of Wisdom, A Modern Interpretation* (Salt Lake City, UT: Deseret News Press, 1938) 15–16.

9 Michael Pollan, *In Defense of Food: An Eater's Manifesto* (New York, NY: Penguin Books, 2008), 90–91.

10 Ibid, 96–97. You can learn more about Dr. Price's findings in his book *Nutrition and Physical Degeneration*, (Lemon Grove, CA: Price-Potter Nutrition; 8th edition, 2008).

11 Widstoe, *The Word of Wisdom, A Modern Interpretation*, 40–41. If you want to read more about the "evil and designs" of the food industry in our generation, see Michael Moss, *Sugar Salt Fat: How the Food Giants Hooked Us* (New York, NY: Random House, 2013).

12 Ezra Taft Benson, *Teachings of Ezra Taft Benson* (Salt Lake City, UT: Bookcraft, 1988), 476–77.

13 For moms who are wondering how to get their families to eat healthier, let me offer one suggestion that I learned the hard way. It's that the more I forced my new nutritional paradigm on my family, the more they resisted and clung to their favorite comfort foods. As I prayed for help, the Spirit gently reminded me that I'd fed my family the typical American diet for many years, and they needed time to adjust to new ways to eating. I was prompted to be patient and take baby steps, meaning I should make small changes when my family and my finances allowed it. Now, several years later, our family has come a long way. My husband and children are much more open to eating healthier foods. So I would simply say, be patient. You don't have to change your family's entire diet all at once. Just rely on the Lord and take it one day at a time.

14 Susan W. Tanner, "The Sanctity of the Body," *Ensign*, November 2005, 13.

15 David A. Bednar, "Ye Are the Temple of God," *Ensign*, September 2001, 14–21.

16 L. Tom Perry, "The Tradition of a Balanced, Righteous Life," *Ensign,* August 2011, 47–53.

17 You can find everything you need for this program at addictionrecovery.lds.org, including the program guide, a meeting locator, and inspirational stories of hope and healing.

Filled with Light

1 "Light," Wikipedia, http://en.wikipedia.org/wiki/Light.

2 Henry B. Eyring, "Walk in the Light," *Ensign*, May 2008, 125.

3 "Enlighten," http://thesaurus.com/browse/enlighten.

4 James E. Talmage, *Jesus the Christ* (Salt Lake City, UT: Deseret Book, 1982), 227.

5 Repentance," LDS Church, Bible Dictionary, LDS Scriptures, 760.

6 Robert D. Hales, "Out of Darkness into His Marvelous Light," *Ensign*, May 2002, 70.

7 James E. Faust, "The Light in Their Eyes," *Ensign*, November 2005, 20.

A Plea for the Next Generation

1 Gilda Radner, *It's Always Something* (New York, NY: Simon & Schuster, 1989), 190–91. Reprinted with the permission of Simon & Schuster Publishing Froupt from IT'S ALWAYS SOMETHING by Gilda Radner. Copyright © 1989 Gilda Radner. Italics added.

2 Jeffrey R. Holland, "To Young Women," *Ensign*, November 2005, 28–30.

3 M. Russell Ballard, "Mothers and Daughters," *Ensign*, May 2010.

4 Ibid.; italics added.

5 Ibid.

About the Author

A first time author, Jaci Green Wightman (pronounced JAY-see) was raised in five different states before meeting her husband during her freshman year of college. Together, they're now enjoying the daunting task of raising seven children born in just eight years. Jaci was thrilled to graduate from BYU–Idaho with a degree in university studies in 2012, twenty-one years after postponing her schooling to start a family. Underneath all her outward busyness, however, Jaci is simply an ordinary woman who discovered an extraordinary Savior. Her greatest joy lies in teaching and testifying of the One who not only changed her heart, but also radically transformed her entire life.

You can contact Jaci at authorjaciwightman@gmail.com.